Death and Fallibility in the Psychoanalytic Encounter

Death and Fallibility in the Psychoanalytic Encounter considers psychoanalysis from a fresh perspective: the therapist's mortality—in at least two senses of the word. That the therapist can die, and is also fallible, can be seen as necessary or even defining components of the therapeutic process. At every moment, the analyst's vulnerability and human limitations underlie the work, something rarely openly acknowledged.

Freud's central insights continue to guide the range of all talking therapies, but they do so somewhat in the manner of a smudged ancestral map. That blur, or degree of confusion, invites new ways of reading. Ellen Pinsky reexamines fundamental principles underlying by-now-dusty terms such as "neutrality," "abstinence," "working through," and the peculiar expression "termination." Pinsky reconsiders—in some measure, hopes to restore—the most essential, humane, and useful components of the original psychoanalytic perspective, guided by the most productive threads in the discipline's still-evolving theory. Freud's most important contribution was arguably to discover (or invent) the psychoanalytic situation itself. This book reflects on central questions pertaining to that extraordinary discovery: What *is* the psychoanalytic situation? How *does* it work (and fail to work)? *Why* does it work?

This book aims to articulate what is fundamental and what we can't do without—the psychoanalytic essence—while neither idealizing Freud nor devaluing his achievement. Historically, Freud has been misread, distorted, maligned, and even, at times, dismissed. Pinsky reappraises his significance with respect to psychoanalytic writers who have extended, and amended, his thinking. Of particular interest are those psychoanalytic thinkers who, like Freud, are not only original thinkers but also great writers—including D. W. Winnicott and Hans Loewald.

Covering a broad range of psychoanalytic paradigms, *Death and Fallibility in the Psychoanalytic Encounter* will bring a fresh understanding of the nature, benefits, and pitfalls of psychoanalysis. It will appeal to psychoanalysts and psychoanalytic psychotherapists and provide superb background and inspiration for anyone working across the entire range of talking therapies.

Ellen Pinsky's articles and reviews have appeared in *The Psychoanalytic Quarterly*, *Journal of the American Psychoanalytic Association*, *American Imago*, *Salmagundi*, and *The Threepenny Review*. She is on the faculty of the Boston Psychoanalytic Society and Institute, where she was awarded the Deutsch Prize for writing.

Psychological Issues

The basic mission of *Psychological Issues* is to contribute to the further development of psychoanalysis as a science, as a respected scholarly enterprise, as a theory of human behavior, and as a therapeutic method.

Over the past 50 years, the series has focused on fundamental aspects and foundations of psychoanalytic theory and clinical practice, as well as on work in related disciplines relevant to psychoanalysis. *Psychological Issues* does not aim to represent or promote a particular point of view. The contributions cover broad and integrative topics of vital interest to all psychoanalysts as well as to colleagues in related disciplines. They cut across particular schools of thought and tackle key issues, such as the philosophical underpinnings of psychoanalysis, psychoanalytic theories of motivation, conceptions of therapeutic action, the nature of unconscious mental functioning, psychoanalysis and social issues, and reports of original empirical research relevant to psychoanalysis. The authors often take a critical stance toward theories and offer a careful theoretical analysis and conceptual clarification of the complexities of theories and their clinical implications, drawing upon relevant empirical findings from psychoanalytic research as well as from research in related fields.

The Editorial Board continues to invite contributions from social/behavioral sciences such as anthropology and sociology, from biological sciences such as physiology and the various brain sciences, and from scholarly humanistic disciplines such as philosophy, law, and ethics. Volumes 1-64 in this series were published by International Universities Press. Volumes 65-69 were published by Jason Aronson.

Routledge titles in this series:

Vol. 74 Manual of Regulation-Focused Psychotherapy for Children (RFP-C) with Externalizing Behaviors: A Psychodynamic Approach
Leon Hoffman, Timothy Rice, & Tracy Prout

Vol. 75 Psychoanalytic Perspectives on Conflict
Edited by Christopher Christian, Morris N. Eagle, & David L. Wolitzky

Vol. 76 Death and Fallibility in the Psychoanalytic Encounter: Mortal Gifts
Ellen Pinsky

"*Death and Fallibility* is a necessary book—necessary for analysts and necessary for the analyses they conduct. In it Ellen Pinsky addresses a long-neglected issue in the practice of psychoanalysis: the analyst's failure to include in the very fiber of the analysis the fact of his or her mortality. This omission is not a minor matter. It arises from deep-seated fears in the analyst that prevent him or her from being fully present in the analysis—facing one's mortality is an integral part of being emotionally present. The book is intelligent, honest, beautifully written, and emotionally moving. What it has to teach is an essential part of the process of becoming an analyst."

—**Thomas Ogden**, author of *Reclaiming Unlived Life* and
This Art of Psychoanalysis

"Inspiring. Ellen Pinsky's essays remind me of why I am interested in psychoanalysis. Loss is the perennial theme, but Pinsky's writing, with its unusually evocative clarity, has something remarkable to add: that there might be something enlivening or intriguing about the inevitable losses in a life is much more than a new note."

—**Adam Phillips**

"Pinsky's eloquent, absorbing and provocative book challenges our comfortable assumptions about what the analyst means to the patient. She corners that elusive experience by scrutinizing—sometimes quite severely—certain limiting situations, such as intermittency of sessions, boundary violations, and the analyst's death in treatment. Pinksy's rich literary references further enlarge our sense of what's at stake, and the awful responsibility of the transference as it touches on issues of life and loss and the nature of human reality. Her bold and unsettling inquiry goes to the heart of psychoanalysis."

—**Lawrence Friedman, M.D.,** Clinical Professor of Psychiatry,
Weill Cornell Medical School

"Ellen Pinsky's gorgeously written *Death and Fallibility* creates wonder and despair. Pinsky describes the fundamental humanness of psychoanalysis through incisive, wide-ranging, and playful literary and theoretical portrayals, always remembering the extraordinary self-knowledge, internal freedom, and sense of being that, perhaps, only analysis can provide. Yet she troubles the reader, asking whether together with this promise there has been, since Freud, something foundationally unethical in the psychoanalytic attitude. Along with human fallibility and mortality, have lack of empathy and the analyst's narcissism historically pervaded analytic work?"

—**Nancy J. Chodorow**, author, *The Reproduction of Mothering,
The Power of Feelings*, and other writings

"In these accessible, poignantly evocative, and stunningly incisive essays, Ellen Pinsky explores the mortal gifts of love and death as they shape each clinical psychoanalytic engagement. She shows technique to be the face of what is most human in humanism, the psychoanalytic situation as a structured invitation that awakens the mobility of desires of falling in love and falling in hate, exposing the immense ethical burden of analyzing. Pulling the reader into a conversation with the analytic masters, this work is an admirable complement to Freud's classical papers on psychoanalytic technique."

—**Warren S. Poland, M.D.,** author of *Melting the Darkness*

"In an arresting prose style, Ellen Pinsky provides evocative reconsiderations on the fundamental principles of psychoanalysis. She draws our attention to the analyst's vulnerability and its effect on the psychoanalytic process. Her perspective is both humane and respectful as she poses ethical dilemmas inherent in psychoanalysis due to the analyst's mortality and human limitations. Reading these linked essays will lead clinicians to a deeper and renewed appreciation of the role of the analyst and the nature of psychoanalytic situation."

—**Judy Kantrowitz**, training and supervising analyst, Boston Psychoanalytic
Society and Institute and author of *The Patient's Impact on the Analyst: Writing about
Patients: responsibilities, risks, and ramifications* and *Myths of Termination:
what patients can teach analyst about endings*

Death and Fallibility in the Psychoanalytic Encounter

Mortal Gifts

Ellen Pinsky

 Routledge
Taylor & Francis Group

LONDON AND NEW YORK

First published 2017
by Routledge
2 Park Square, Milton Park, Abingdon, Oxon OX14 4RN

and by Routledge
711 Third Avenue, New York, NY 10017

Routledge is an imprint of the Taylor & Francis Group, an informa business

British Library Cataloguing in Publication Data
A catalogue record for this book is available from the British Library

Library of Congress Cataloging in Publication Data
A catalog record has been requested for this book

ISBN: 978-1-138-92868-8 (hbk)
ISBN: 978-1-138-92869-5 (pbk)
ISBN: 978-1-315-68139-9 (ebk)

Typeset in Times New Roman
by Deanta Global Publishing Services, Chennai, India

With love and respect for all the good guardians,

through the generations

and

In memory of Dr. S. Joseph Nemetz

Contents

Acknowledgments   x

Introduction   1

1 Physic Himself Must Fade   6

2 The Potion   26

3 The Olympian Delusion   44

4 The Instrument   69

5 Mirrors and Monsters   92

Epilogue   119

References   122

Index   131

Acknowledgments

I am indebted to many teachers, colleagues, and friends for their encouragement and criticism.

Colleagues who have most centrally challenged and supported me include Stephen Bernstein, Fred Busch, Lisa Carbone, Nancy Chodorow, Lawrence Friedman, Richard Gottlieb, Pam Greenberg, Alexandra Harrison, Sybil Houlding, Judy Kantrowitz, Catherine Kimble, Jane Kite, Tony Kris, Alfred Margulies, Karen Melikian, Janet Noonan, Shelley Orgel, Thomas Ogden, Jonathan Palmer, Ava Penman, Adam Phillips, Warren Poland, Cordelia Schmidt-Hellerau, Jan Seriff, Pam Wine, Peter Wohlauer, and Judy Yanof.

I'm also grateful for the generous wisdom and support of Jill Bloom, Robert Boyers, Peg Boyers, Leslie Epstein, David Ferry, Louise Gluck, Wendy Lesser, Phillip Lopate, Jim McMichael, Murray Schwartz, Dawn Skorczewski, Karen Smolens, David Thorburn, and David Wolitzky. A special debt to Ellen Blumenthal.

My deepest gratitude to my husband Robert.

The Lawrence Friedman epigraph featured at the start of Chapter 5 is taken from his article "What Is Psychoanalysis?" in *Psychoanalytic Quarterly*, 75(3) (2006): 689–713. Reprinted by permission of John Wiley & Sons, Inc.

Excerpts from "Childhood and Poetry" from *Neruda and Vallejo* by Pablo Neruda, translated by Robert Bly. Copyright 1993 by Robert Bly. Reprinted with the permission of the translator.

Excerpts from Donald Winnicott's "The Observation of Infants in a Set Situation" in *International Journal of Psychoanalysis*, 22 (1941): 229–249. Copyright 1941. Reprinted with the permission of John Wiley & Sons, Inc.

Introduction[1]

Lord, what fools these mortals be!
—Puck, *A Midsummer-Night's Dream*, III, 2

I will consider psychoanalysis through a quite specific topic: the therapist's mortality, in at least two senses of that word. The therapist is fallible, and also can die: these may be seen as necessary or even defining components of the psychoanalytic process. At every moment, the analyst's human vulnerability and mortal limitations underlie the work.

That underlying reality can clarify fundamental principles, refreshing such by-now-dusty terms as "neutrality," "abstinence," "working-through," and the peculiar expression "termination." Those terms are illuminated by recalling their original context: as Sigmund Freud was well aware, the doctor is fallible as well as vulnerable.

I reconsider, and even in some measure hope to restore, the most essential, humane, and useful components of the original psychoanalytic perspective, guided by what I find to be significant currents in the discipline's still-evolving theory. If Freud's most important contribution was to discover (or, as some prefer, to invent) the psychoanalytic situation, this book reflects on central questions pertaining to that extraordinary discovery: How does it work (and fail to work)? *Why* does it work? What does it offer?

No social institution is more peculiar to the twentieth century than psychoanalysis, the "talking cure" shaped by Freud a little over 100 years ago. Resisted and suspect as a bold upstart in the early years, then climbing to immense cultural prominence in the first half of the twentieth century, by century's turn psychoanalysis was beleaguered: a superannuated dowager under attack, lagging behind new medical technologies, new social and economic realities. Moreover, while from the outside the social place of psychoanalysis (and its offshoots) remains ambiguous, from the inside the basic philosophy of the talking cure remains vague.

And yet this unusual professional arrangement retains its prominence, even centrality, despite revisionisms, evolutions, adaptations, withering critiques, and formidable rivals. Why?

Two people meet alone in a room regularly, over time, and they talk, their relationship itself an object of scrutiny. No one had ever before thought of asking two people to engage one another in quite this way. Nor is there agreement about how such inspection works to benefit the one who pays. Only urgent needs can have allowed so strange and vaguely defined an institution to survive and even flourish, in so many mutations, and cultural stereotypes, for so long. Why, like the man on the desert island, has it become a stock locale for one-panel cartoons? What is the appeal, or what need is filled?

The striking resilience of the talking cure, its fallibility, and its dilemma of definition all have roots in the mortal nature of human beings. The therapist is mortal both literally (he or she can die) and figuratively (he or she is fallible). We can detect the appeal and utility, as well as the imperfection, of talking therapy in that double limitation. The psychoanalytic situation itself is defined by carefully structured limitation that creates freedom, by restriction that creates range: a "No, we will not touch" that says "Yes, you may freely speak your desire." Only an imperfect being can energize this extraordinary offering, as no god or robot could do.

When Shakespeare's Antony reports to Cleopatra that her rival Fulvia is dead, Cleopatra asks a rhetorical question we might ask about the psychoanalyst: "Can Fulvia die?" (*Antony and Cleopatra*, I, 3).

Suppose that this actually happens. Consider the patient's role at the late therapist's public memorial: the ambiguities and uncomfortable exposure in the social realm of what that social realm has sanctioned but also segregated. The patient's awkward presence may recall that of the mistress at a funeral, the loneliness and social derangement epitomizing the peculiarity of psychotherapy as a social encounter: ordinary manners do not cover the case.

Figuratively, mortality is a metonymy for mere humanity. We all die, and know that we will die: a knowledge that embodies and sometimes ennobles our imperfection. Uniquely among vendor-consumer relationships, imperfection is a requisite for the therapeutic process. Mortality (sometimes along with ordinary defects such as folly, self-delusion, greed, lustfulness) pervades the psychoanalytic relationship, its risks and possibilities, its useful fictions and awkward truths, its paradoxes and its accomplishments. More pointedly than the funeral, the therapeutic session offers a place where something may be gained from the possibly disjunctive, unique mingling of actual life and a stylized reflection of that life.

On the vendor side of the relationship, the analyst's mortal imperfection has been variously bracketed—controlled or held implicit, suppressed or even denied outright. Why? The situation, intentionally tilted, invites a particular kind of intensity, called the transference, and its reciprocal force, the countertransference. The persisting growth of the countertransference literature indicates the magnitude of that force, as do controversies—now become almost formulaic—about therapeutic action: for example, "Is it interpretation or the relationship that's mutative?" or "Is it a one-person or a two-person psychology?"—as if "the reality" can be reduced to any such either/or toggle.

That the "talking cure" is problematic was learned at the start, with the unruly power of forces released by the process apparent in the egregious transgressions among Freud's early disciples. Freud's *Papers on Technique* (1911–1915) charts his struggle to understand the complexity of his own discovery, including its dangers. Some would say that Freud truly becomes a psychoanalyst only with the "Postscript to Dora" (1905), where he unequivocally locates transference at the center of the psychoanalytic process. *Papers on Technique* follows shortly. Many decades later, Lawrence Friedman (1988) begins *The Anatomy of Psychotherapy* with this sentence: "Most psychotherapists sense that their work is vague and its image misleading, and they are occasionally reminded that they have no authentic place in society because society doesn't know what they are up to" (ix). The truth of this statement makes the very survival of the method something of a marvel. One is reminded of Boccaccio's tale of the Jew who, seeing the scandalous goings-on at the Vatican, decides to convert because only a true religion could survive such things.

Not only can the therapist die, and not only *will* he die, but the truism carries an even more uncomfortable corollary—at any moment (which really means, at *every* moment) he might. No one likes to think about this universal fact, or can think about it for long, and most of the time we don't think about it at all. Forgetting—or, in Freud's term, repression—is also on the side of life, just as the River Lethe has two banks, one demarking the realm of the dead, the other that of the living. Endangering—yet, I believe, also enabling—every therapeutic engagement is the analyst's mortal nature.

I came to this subject of the analyst's mortality through an event that transformed truism to stunning fact: my own therapist's sudden death—a painful but peculiar loss, like no other. My family and friends, and the profession, were generous and sympathetic as I grieved for my dead therapist. Still, grief was amplified by confusion and isolation, and complicated by a sense of absurdity too: no one close to me knew this person to whom I felt so close and spoke so freely and privately. In melancholia, in contrast to mourning, writes Freud (1917), the bereaved one "knows *whom* he has lost but not *what* he has lost in him" (245, emphasis in original). However, even after dealing explicitly with object loss in "Mourning and Melancholia," Freud never referred in his writing to the loss of the analyst or the meaning of that loss for the patient and the analytic process (Blum 1989: 279). The loss of my analyst had to be mourned, and the absence filled. But what had I lost? To take its measure I also had to wonder, What had I been given?

In his essay "George Herbert—the Giver and the Gift," the literary scholar William Nestrick (1975) writes: "The only appropriate gift is discovered to be a thing inseparable from the giver, for the very reason that, in his role as giver, man can only give himself" (189). The child's valentine, the pearl necklace, the homemade cake, the work of art, the donated kidney, the endowment of a hospital wing—each offering gestures toward another, either imagined or real, and betokens a relationship between people. Perhaps Freud (1914a) has something like this in mind when he writes in "On Narcissism" that the individual "does actually carry on a twofold existence: one to serve his own purposes and the other as a link in a chain":

> The individual himself regards sexuality as one of his own ends; whereas from another point of view he is an appendage to his germ-plasm, at whose disposal he puts his energies in return for a bonus of pleasure. *He is the mortal vehicle of a (possibly) immortal substance*—like the inheritor of an entailed property, who is only the temporary holder of an estate which survives him.
>
> (Freud 1914a: 78, emphasis added)

Man's "estate" is also of course his human condition, and his "germ-plasm" a necessary part of the human exchange, if there are to be literal generations. Might Freud's "(possibly) immortal substance" also be understood as an offering related to the transmission of culture? The gift (soma and psyche) is mortal; the donor is imperfect as well as transitory. On such a conception, the analyst's good enough interpretation—the words that convey the intention to understand—is a gift of the self, with the unique limitations of one particular soul.

The therapeutic offering is, in this light, a *mortal gift*. Its source is not divine nor quite scientific, nor is the gift eternal but subject to time and loss, just as the therapeutic work itself, like all human growth, proceeds by increments of separation and loss. But, ultimately, the gift—or offering— is a mystery, and all the more valued, in being received, for its relation to imperfection and to transience. Limitation, defining our condition, is what makes anything—or everything—human possible.

Note

1 This text originally appeared, in a slightly different form, as part of "Physic Himself Must Fade," *American Imago*, 69(1) (2012): 29–56. Reprinted with permission.

Chapter 1

Physic Himself Must Fade[1]

On love, on grief, on every human thing,
Time sprinkles Lethe's water with his wing.
—Walter Savage Landor

Limited as a human being, limitless in the patient's casting of him, the analyst is a magnetic presence almost without explicit dimension: a shadow figure, known yet not known, who exists largely for the patient's invention. As if that weren't odd enough, this therapeutic relationship, unlike many other deep relationships, emphasizes ending as a register of its success. Therapeutic intimacy intends from the outset to end, just as each hour ends, foreshadowing that finality.

Composed of discrete time-limited segments, this special form of discovery and intimacy has for its goal a restorative separation, the analyst becoming, in Loewald's terms, a "presence in absence" (1978: 180), the relationship internalized over time. A magnet for reawakened desires, fears, hopes, and hatreds, the analyst, a mortal reservoir, performs his (or her) function by surviving, within a construct, each of the patient's idiosyncratic uses of him. He isn't supposed to die—though the relationship, in its peculiar jargon, is supposed to "terminate."

Freud's newly invented professional figure is an ordinary person serving an artificial or "as-if" role in a fiduciary engagement. Can a chimera die? When the fairy Puck says, "What fools these mortals be," the Shakespeare character's "mortal" seems to indicate human folly as well as vulnerability. The folly, the vulnerability, and the certainty of death apply to all humans, including doctors and their arts of medicine. In the words of Shakespeare's contemporary Thomas Nashe:

Rich men, trust not in wealth,
Gold cannot buy you health;

Physic himself must fade;
All things to end are made,
The plague full swift goes by;
I am sick, I must die—
Lord, have mercy on us
  (from "In Time of Plague")

To these two profoundly traditional notions about the human condition—
that man is a fool and he also dies—we can contrast Donald Winnicott's
well-known aphorism, "The analyst survives." Puck, a kind of god, speaks
words written by one mortal and performed by another. The play, like
the immortal Puck, lives, though William Shakespeare is dead. A similar
intersection of the ordinary and the uncanny, the actual and the simulated,
is at the very heart of the therapeutic relationship, with its flaws and benefits: a gift that is mortal in its origin as well as its nature.

  A therapist's humanness is of course no more extricable from his or her
professional functioning than is the human idiosyncrasy of any parent or
teacher (or any role of guardianship) separable from their acquired skills.
Rather, that humanness is the foundation upon which the work rests. But
unlike the mores of child care, evolved and shifting over centuries, and
unlike the teacher's humanness embedded in the culture of pedagogy, the
odd activity of the analyst is a twentieth-century invention. An artifice,
psychotherapy functions by offering a safe, delimited illusion, like a play.
The vehicle of attraction derives its energy from a human being, someone fallible as well as vulnerable in that benign fostered illusion. Freud's
stratagem starts with love:

> The process of cure is accomplished in a relapse into love, if we com-
> bine all the many components of sexual instinct under the term "love";
> and such a relapse is indispensable, for the symptoms on account of
> which the treatment has been undertaken are nothing other than pre-
> cipitates of earlier struggles connected with repression or the return of
> the repressed, and they can only be resolved and washed away by a
> fresh high tide of the same passions.
>
>   (1907: 90)

What kind of love is this "fresh high tide of the same passions"? Freud
(1916–1917) describes the development of transference: "By this we mean
a transference of feelings on to the person of the physician, because we do

not believe that the situation in the treatment can account for the origin of such feelings" (442). Freud (1910) is quite clear from the start about the universality of this "transference," a phenomenon that "arises spontaneously in all human relationships, just as it does between the patient and the physician" (51).

But unlike other relationships, the analytic doctor in the consulting room puts that phenomenon, purposefully intensified by the structured situation, to a particular use:

> In every psycho-analytic treatment … the strange phenomenon that is known as "transference" makes its appearance. The patient, that is to say, directs toward the physician a degree of affectionate feeling (mingled, often enough, with hostility) which is based on no real relation between them and which … can only be traced back to old wishful phantasies of the patient's which have become unconscious. Thus the part of the patient's emotional life which he can no longer recall to memory is re-experienced by him in his relation to the physician; and it is only this re-experiencing in the "transference" that convinces him of the existence and power of these unconscious sexual impulses.
>
> (Freud 1910: 51)

Making an analogy to chemistry, Freud captures the heat of this transference process fueled by memory and desire, as well as the doctor's role in the "reaction"—an implicit potential combustion:

> [The patient's] symptoms, to take an analogy from chemistry, are precipitates of earlier experiences in the sphere of love (in the widest sense of the word), and it is only in the *raised temperature* of his experience of the transference that they can be resolved and reduced to other psychical products. In this reaction the physician … plays the part of a *catalytic ferment*, which temporarily attracts to itself the affects liberated in the process.
>
> (Freud 1910: 51, emphasis added)

It's easy enough to see the danger in this artificial realm of "raised temperature," a stage purposely tilted to court "fresh high tides" of intense feeling—the past brought to life in the present—with the analyst in the role of love object but also in the position of guardianship and responsibility: desired, and protective. These are the same "highly explosive forces" to which Freud refers in his great essay "Observations on Transference-Love" (1915), describing the circumstance whereby the patient quite naturally—"as any other mortal woman might" (1915a: 159)—falls in love with the doctor. And Freud here poses a fundamental, imperative question: "But how is the analyst to behave in order not to come to grief over this situation?" (163).

That is: what is the analyst to do in response to this "falling in love in the transference" (Freud 1915a: 162), the result, precisely, of a calculated invitation—arguably (in some technical sense) a seduction? The idea of "transference" thus provides, brilliantly, both possibility of cure, in real life, and a necessary safety for the doctor: a protective distance on that special stage. Vehicle, safety, and danger—transference is all in one, the mortal analyst playing the part of a "catalytic ferment."

Although Freud's narrow focus here is the danger of sexual exploitation, his question—How is the analyst to behave?—has implications for the entire relationship between patient and doctor. Freud's (1915a) formulation, necessary but fateful, places the analyst's conduct in the oddest of categories: "The course the analyst must pursue," he writes, "is one for which there is no model in real life" (166). According to this remarkable prescription, the analyst, in managing the transferential relationship, must behave in no known manner, according to no known code. This exceptional affective element may be likened to a potion (as I call it in Chapter 2), a magical concoction with both medicinal and poisonous potential. The doctor must not follow his (or her) merely mortal nature by giving in to the heated situation: "The treatment must be carried out in abstinence," the analyst neither gratifying nor suppressing "the patient's craving for love" but instead treating it "as something unreal" (Freud 1915a: 166).

Abstinence, then, is a fundamental principle of treatment: reliably neither seductive nor seduced, the analyst abstains, his appetites withheld, his expression of feelings in check.

If, as Freud says, transference is a universal phenomenon, then all human relationships, however "real," are also in part imagined—imbued with feelings associated with early love objects. However, the treatment relationship itself, Freud emphasizes, is unique: it has no model. But can this really be *true*? Does the analytic doctor—unlike the mother, the father, the lover, the friend, the teacher, the plumber, the mail carrier—resist every other form of social behavior, every inclination of ordinary human nature, restricting himself (or herself) exclusively to analyzing the forces stirred in the transference?

Perhaps Freud means that for none of these other objects of transference is the position as fully stylized (or perhaps also as attractive, magnetic, even addictive): a stringency limiting reciprocal action and seductive behavior—the analyst's abstinence—along with a non-judgmental receptiveness to everything the patient expresses—the analyst's benevolent neutrality. The analyst neither criticizes nor approves, supplies neither "yes" nor "no." Instead, he interprets, putting words to the patient's wishes whose object he is. In this way the analyst takes a meta-position: the analytic "as-if," the stance based on abstinence and neutrality.

None of this is to say that the patient's "craving for love" isn't real; nor does it mean that the analyst is unresponsive, quite the contrary: human nature assumes response to another's longing. But the analytic doctor doesn't act on that response as he or she might in ordinary life. In becoming the object of the patient's desire, the analyst is required to suspend his or her own nature, in a balance that recognizes both human response and fellow feeling (how else to understand the patient but through fellow feeling?) but at the same time prohibits enacting them. This is an extraordinary demand on an ordinary person. Both people abstain from direct sexual activity, but the patient's task—to give free expression to his or her cravings—is very different from the analyst's task. The analyst suspends his appetites, though not empathic understanding, and instead the doctor analyzes: a tactic, and an attitude, only intensifying the patient's longing.

We may see implicit here the fundamental paradox of abstinence as *alluring*: the principle of abstinence protects but, by design, also heats the treatment crucible, thus conflating the ethical and the technical. No idea is more central to the analytic project than this one. In 1950, building on Freud's propositions in *Papers on Technique*, Ida Macalpine (1950) writes that the analyst's moral integrity "becomes a safeguard for the patient to proceed with analysis: it is a technical device and not a moral precept" (527). The analyst's moral integrity, in this tough-minded view, is a necessary condition in two senses. On the one hand, treatment is possible only with moral integrity as a given condition; in this meaning, it is a mechanism, or device, an additional feature of the bounded frame, like the time limit or the fee the patient pays. On the other hand, moral integrity is a human condition or state of being; in this meaning, it is an ideal human attribute achievable only partially by an always-particular, always-striving, always-imperfect person: that is, a mortal being.

I believe Freud (1915a) means something similar when he advises that the analyst let it be seen that "he is proof against every temptation" (166), though of course he may feel temptation, along with the full range of emotion, as is part of one's humanness. The trustworthiness of the non-perfect being—the analyst's trustworthiness—is something attained, and in that sense (again) it is a mortal gift. This gift is always being tested, necessarily so. The analyst strives to hold an uncomfortable, contradictory position, the role for which there is no model: the analyst is "an actor inside and outside of a passionate, but nevertheless merely virtual, drama" (Friedman 2006: 704).

Characterizing the intensity of the treatment situation, Richard Almond (2011) writes that "the psychoanalytic relationship has a charismatic quality" (1136). Almond is referring in part to Freud's (1912a) statement in "The Dynamics of Transference": "We do not understand why transference is so much more intense with neurotic subjects in analysis" (101). Crediting Chodorow (2010), who invokes the social theorist George Simmel on characteristics pertaining to dyads, Almond writes:

> What Simmel, by way of Chodorow, offers as an answer to Freud's question about intensity is that the private, dyadic setup of analysis in itself creates an emotional hothouse … The intensity of the psychoanalytic relationship … derive[s] from intrinsic characteristics of dyads that are secluded, that meet frequently, and that are not highly scripted.
>
> (2011: 1134)

Another paradox is embedded here: in a situation that is, by its structure, inherently seductive for both people, the analyst must strive, in the interest of Macalpine's "technical device," to be non-seductive and unseduced. Or, to put the paradox another way: virtual seduction is necessarily an element in the therapeutic process and must not be the actual outcome.

To resist acting on his or her "ordinary human nature" in the face of the patient's awakened desire and intensity of pressure, then, is one definition of the analytic doctor's professional role.

But is the analyst then *out of* nature, like the immortal bird of Yeats' "Sailing to Byzantium"? What will the doctor's manner, and manners, be in this fundamentally paradoxical encounter, a relationship that is intimate yet professional, professional yet barely social? And what manners prevail above and beyond the analyst's powers or life span? If Freud's "no model in real life" leaves the analyst without clear definition in the world of ordinary social behavior, do we locate the doctor in "unreal" life, a designation that might suggest an Olympus where no one really dies? The analyst, unseen during the work, is something *like* a ghost—on "the other side," with bracketing helloes and goodbyes.

Freud never let go the warning, writing, now near the end of his life, about the double-edged power of the transferential relationship: "[It is] a factor of undreamt-of importance," he writes, "on the one hand an instrument of irreplaceable value and on the other hand a source of serious dangers" (1940: 174–175). One might wonder if Freud's phrasing here—"undreamt-of importance"—includes a concession, marking his own struggle over the years to conceive the "factor": did Freud himself *under*perceive the power, including the destructive potential, of the transferential relationship?

The psychoanalytic situation is indeed an audacious endeavor, for a time placing one human being *as if* at the center of another's emotional life. The question follows: What is the patient's protection in such a daring professional encounter that purposely courts risk? Donald Winnicott writes:

> In doing psycho-analysis I aim at:
>   Keeping alive
>   Keeping well
>   Keeping awake
>   I aim at being myself and behaving myself.
>   Having begun an analysis I expect to continue with it, to survive it, and to end it.
>
> (1962: 166)

This compact credo suggests that the analyst must try to behave (though there is no model for his behavior) and he must survive (though he is merely mortal). He may neither misbehave nor die. But whether Winnicott has in mind here the analyst's literal or figurative "keeping alive" (or both), he is in effect elaborating on Freud's idea of the analyst having no model. With this systematic striving for fundamental, even minimal, goals—keeping alive, well, awake—Winnicott, like Freud, is proposing a guide for the analyst's conduct: an analytic attitude and the doctor's professional role.

Fifty years earlier, in *Papers on Technique* (1911–1915), Freud elaborates technical recommendations for conducting treatment with the ideals of "anonymity," "abstinence," and "neutrality." Developed out of clinical necessity, as Freud and his early followers experienced the power of the transferential relationship, such guides, deliberately elastic and spacious, were never intended as narrow rules. These guiding terms nevertheless present first principles: both systematic procedure and ethical precept. Freud's language for describing this analytic stance differs from Winnicott's "alive, well, and awake," but Freud's analyst, like Winnicott's, is always humanly present, and not separate from what he does technically. Freud's preoccupations in *Papers on Technique* attest to such an understanding.

Freud's much maligned and misunderstood term "neutrality," for example, indicates a receptivity that has nothing to do with coldness or indifference. The analyst is self-restrained and open-minded, he is non-intrusive but affectively involved—far different from the trite caricature of the silent doctor created by later generations. Perhaps part of Winnicott's purpose, writing in mid-century, is to retrieve Freud's dehumanized analyst from encrusting stereotypes.

As with Freud, the aims for Winnicott's analyst include "being myself," an allusion to his individual personal presence. Winnicott's analyst, in merely keeping alive, well, and awake, and by surviving without misbehavior the patient's various uses of him, including attempts to seduce or destroy him, actually accomplishes something. Winnicott further humanizes the analyst by bluntly including his hatred. The analyst who is "alive, well, and awake" will also recognize his countertransference hate (see Winnicott 1949). But good conduct is not automatic: good conduct is achieved, through systematic striving. The person who serves as a transference magnet (Freud's "catalytic ferment") can only aim at "being himself" and at "behaving himself," as ideals. By maintaining, well enough, the *function as analyst*—however much it may be with "no model"—the analyst guides safe treatment.

Like Freud, Winnicott understands that these aims are conceivable only virtually, within a construct: psychotherapy *is* unreal life—precisely—and the analyst maintains that analytic function by serving an artificial and contingent role, the patient making of him what he or she will. This is Freud's analyst as reflecting "mirror." The analyst's conduct is at the same time always rooted in awareness that, while artifice gives him potency and protection, he is at every moment subject to real life too. That is, he is morally and physically imperfect because he is human. At every moment, the analyst can die—or misbehave—and sometimes does. What's more, Winnicott (1969) says that, within the artifice, behaving well, surviving the patient's attacks without retaliation, may be more important than that he not die: "even the actual death of the analyst," writes Winnicott, "is not as bad as the development in the analyst of a change of attitude toward retaliation" (714).

Perhaps Winnicott means here that dying, unlike retaliation, is not a breach of neutrality—the doctor's professional attitude. In other words, the virtual death, wherein the *function* is lost, may be more destructive to the treatment than the actual one, an idea I will return to throughout this book.

The analyst, in safe-keeping the position of analyst, becomes a human medium, serving as *all* other people, but with a disciplined attention and safety attained by this one, particular mortal in this one, peculiar situation. An angel—a creature of pure reason—could not represent, or embody, all of humanity because we mortals, unlike the angels, are capable of reason only intermittently. The good enough analyst, in managing this complex role, may humbly aspire to a reliable character, but perfection, like the invulnerable body, belongs to the gods. The power of psychoanalytic treatment resides in the transferential relationship—Freud's "factor of undreamt-of importance"—the *model* for the analyst's behavior both universal and non-judgmental as a mirror.

...

And what of the second person in the room? On entering treatment, the patient agrees to speak with candor, putting into words all that he or she thinks and feels, concealing nothing from the analyst—this is the "fundamental rule," a charge to speak freely unlike any exchange in the ordinary social realm. In this unusual freedom we may hear echoed Freud's "no model in real life," focusing here not on the analyst's role and task but on the task for the patient, whose position also has "no model." It is "a complex injunction," writes André Green (2005), "for the patient is not only asked to say everything, including what seems to be the most absurd, the most contingent, *but to do nothing*" (33, emphasis in original).

The patient of course can't foresee the anxieties and risks attending this pledge of candor. Ana-Maria Rizzuto evokes the force and sweep of the psychoanalytic process:

> which has the dynamic potential to reawaken every past desire for communication and love, protection and admiration, that the patient has experienced in the course of his life. Together with the desire and the hope come the fears of past rejections and failures, traumas and life injuries.
>
> (1995: 5)

Every patient, in embarking on a psychoanalysis, risks an intimacy and an exposure that can't be anticipated. Nor is the patient likely at the outset to measure the insular nature of this most private of professional relationships. The patient expects the joint labor to bear fruit, the analyst remaining until an agreed-on ending. That implicit promise of constancy makes risk tolerable: the paid helper will be there for guidance, reliable to the end.

It goes without saying that this summary doesn't mean to blame the individual therapist who becomes sick or dies for his human condition. The analyst, like all who assume roles of guardianship, knows that he "has implicitly promised what he cannot possibly guarantee" (Ogden 1997: 11). But the ever-present clinical reality that the analyst could at any time fail because he is only human raises theoretical questions. Because the therapeutic contract by its nature fosters emotional dependence on a professional caregiver, it would seem an obvious responsibility of the profession to look hard in an institutional as well as theoretical sense at this contingency as a clinical matter. The loss, after all, moves onto center stage a new problem for the patient, one imposed by what was supposed to be the vehicle of help. Without responsibility—which is to say, answerability—there is a catastrophic breach of the therapeutic contract. What is the patient's recourse in such a catastrophe? I ask the question not with protocols in mind (those, I believe, are essentially easy), but in the sense, again, of *theoria*: to behold, and *to see into* the problem.

In this respect the profession has been slow, even unconscionably slow, to take responsibility for the power of its method. Robert Gardner (1983) refers to the "failure of psychoanalysts to practice the self inquiry they preach" (6). The analyst's job—according to Winnicott—is in some sense to survive; the patient's task includes a "self inquiry" that requires an unwavering examination of the most frightening truths about himself, an unveiling of all he would conceal. How do we reconcile the fact that therapists get sick and die with the fact that, historically, little has been written either about such loss or the underlying realities it raises—a remarkable failure of collective "self inquiry"?

As I will try to show, not only does the psychoanalytic literature on the illness and death of the therapist reveal an historical avoidance of the subject, but a striking skittishness characterizes the small (though growing) body of contemporary papers. Themes of omission and denial emerge repeatedly: an "affect-filled silence" (Schwartz and Silver 1990: 2).[2] When the subject is addressed, the chief focus is almost always on the analyst's predicament, the analyst's decisions about what will benefit the patient, the analyst's judgment about the effect of an intervention, but there is silence on the matter of his or her own vulnerability. The patient's voice throughout the literature is faint, the patient's dilemma downplayed or absent. Here we may find another striking paradox: the goal of the treatment relationship is to free the patient to speak, but in the particular instance of the analyst's death, the patient's voice tends to be silenced. Ultimately, as in any human relationship, Loewald (1980 [1970]) writes, "the truth of human beings is revealed in their interrelatedness" (298).

Why should consideration of the most fundamental reality, that we all die, be suppressed in psychoanalytic discourse, an attenuation that seems more an act of commission than omission? Is it a repression? A suppression? In what mix? One factor of course is universal: death terrifies us all into silence.

But professional responsibility isn't abrogated by universality. The common retort that psychoanalysts, like everyone else, are afraid of death, doesn't answer the specific question: Why is the urgent matter of the therapist's mortality, in *particular*, neglected? What hidden fears underlie this avoidance? Along with dread, perhaps its complementary opposite, grandiosity of thinking—"I am above death, I am larger than it"—plays a part as well. Perhaps a more troubling possibility even than the analyst's dread or grandiosity: does the inadequacy of the literature reflect an aggression—the analyst's wish, in Winnicott's terms, to retaliate? On such a notion, the analyst is full of hatred, and vengeful.

For what might the analyst wish to retaliate?

Possibly for the raised temperatures of the transferential relationship, whose powerful forces were only gradually discovered by Freud, and necessarily rediscovered by every analytic therapist—a trial by fire for the figure who plays the part of Freud's "catalytic ferment." Possibly for the stress of the patient's craving and insistent demands, as though to say, "I hate you for all your mewling and puking in my arms." Or, is the retaliation a vengeance for the analyst's less than total importance?—a fantasy, for example, "Only *I* can treat you," a savior fantasy. Like Huck Finn, in relishing his own funeral, is there a universal fantasy of revenge?—"The more chaos, then the more I'm missed. *Now* you'll appreciate me!" Or, the retaliation may be driven less by fear of dying than that of living on within the patient though no longer present. It may require a selfless quality to respond generously to being needed (and loved or hated) when one is already dead—"A little like being an organ donor," as a colleague remarked, "who doesn't make it and resents the recipient's pleasure in the new kidney."

Whatever combination we choose among the possibilities (the reader will likely add more), as complex and various as motives underlying any human behavior, the silence or squeamishness in the literature must have meaning. The itemizing of explanations itself recalls Winnicott's marvelous list in his paper "Hate in the Counter-Transference" (1949): "some" of the reasons (he elaborates eighteen!) why "a mother hates her baby, even a boy" (73). This shocker is perhaps a playful poke at Freud as well as a provocation of the reader. Winnicott concludes this comic tour de force: "He excites her but frustrates, she mustn't eat him or trade in sex with him." The mother, according to Winnicott, "has to be able to tolerate hating her baby without doing anything about it" (74). We might call this non-retaliatory maternal acceptance—a form of benign passivity—another instance of the gift made kinetic by its imperfection.

Winnicott (1949) makes the analogy to psychotherapy explicit: "in the ultimate stages of the analysis, even of a normal person [he means a "neurotic" person], the analyst must find himself in a position comparable to that of the mother of a new-born baby" (74). Perhaps Winnicott's riff here is provocative, even demeaning, throughout, in part expressing his hatred of his own patients and of the profession (see Kahr 2015). Winnicott's eighteenth and climactic reason—"He excites her but frustrates, she mustn't eat him or trade in sex with him"—calls to mind (is it deliberate?) the psychoanalytic history of sexual transgression in the clinical setting: both analyst and mother must tolerate destructive and exciting impulses. The passage may flag also Winnicott's own well-documented struggle to stay within the treatment frame.

Winnicott, like Freud, understands that the analyst will necessarily experience a range of feelings in the heat (which he has by his position provoked) of the transference. In playing the role of a catalytic ferment, the analyst is protected by formal elements imbedded in the carefully structured arrangement. These are similar, Winnicott says, to the way the mother is helped by the songs she sings to soothe her demanding and hateful baby: the lullaby "Rock-a-Bye Baby," for example, where wind blows, boughs break, cradles (and babies) fall. Winnicott points to the end of the hour as among the formal means whereby the analyst expresses hate for the patient; and, he adds, "I get paid." Payment and time limits, parts of the analytic setting—those conditions that make treatment possible—may elicit strong feeling and at the same time make that intensity more bearable for both people. "The professional attitude is rather like symbolism," Winnicott (1960) writes elsewhere, "in that it assumes a *distance between analyst and patient* (161, emphasis in original).

The mundane, regular, time-limited hour and the analyst's ordinary act of interpretation—the one a defining temporal boundary, the other a defining formulation—are protective as well as internally structuring. The patient's feelings for the analyst, called up in the process of transference, must be bounded by a functional loss or formal limit. The hour ends, or the analyst interprets. (That defining limitation is the subject of Chapter 4, "The Instrument.") What the patient has of the analyst is always circumscribed, or endangered, which only increases its value—in a way similar to what Freud (1916a) says to the pessimistic poet in "On Transience." The transience of nature's beauty involves no loss in its worth: "On the contrary, an increase!" he declares. "Transience value is scarcity value in time" (305). In "Observations on Transference-Love," Freud (1915a) is careful to warn, with his own characteristic comic sense, that the analyst "must recognize that the patient's falling in love is induced by the analytic situation and is not to be attributed to the charms of his own person" (160–161).

I have said that the analyst offers a mortal gift. The Greek *kharisma*, a divine gift, comes from the gods, a definition suggesting strictures and reservations. The phenomenon of transference love, says Freud (1915a), "signifies [for the doctor] a valuable piece of enlightenment and a useful warning against any tendency to a counter-transference which may be present in his own mind" (160). The psychoanalytic situation is, in Almond's terms, a charismatic arrangement, inherently endowing the analyst with allure. Drawing on Jerome Frank (Frank and Frank 1961), Almond (2011) writes about "specialness": "In treatments varying from psychoanalysis to shamanistic healing, [Frank] observed the recurrence of specialness. The healer needs to believe in the power of his or her theory and technique; the subjects must believe in the healer's special capacities" (1136). In other words, a charismatic element is structural. However, the cool, smiling irony of Freud's "not to be attributed to the charms of his own person" indicates a limit—a recognition that the doctor is mortal in both senses. The idea of a *personal* charisma beyond the structural is redundant, but beyond that, defective: a charismatic analyst, as I'll argue in Chapter 2, is a contradiction in terms, at least in the clinical setting.

This is one of few direct references Freud makes to the analyst's "counter-transference," although the countertransference—those temptations and dangers of the doctor's reciprocal falling in love—is also the essay's subject, clearly implicit in Freud's deflating warnings against it. The patient's love is provoked by the analytic situation and it is the analyst who sets the process in motion and is responsible also for limiting it and protecting it. Winnicott's "Hate in the Counter-Transference" may be read as a commentary on Freud's 1915 paper: where Freud seems to say, "I don't know what to do with the love," Winnicott writes, "I don't know what to do with the hate" (Winnicott, "Trips into Partnership," quoted by Kahr 2015: 69). Winnicott's paper on countertransference hate, writes Kahr (2015), "helps us, nonetheless, to understand the potential for enacting one's hatred unconsciously" (78). As complement to Freud's earlier paper on transference love, Winnicott's essay makes clear that the doctor's reciprocal falling in love, if acted upon, becomes a betrayal of trust rooted in delusion: this superior, would-be charismatic form of hate is scorn.

The analyst's neutrality and abstinence, as conceived by Freud, are forms of *presence*, not absence. In contrast with everything put in place to make treatment possible—the construct of transference, the structured, bounded, limited nature of the exchange—is the phenomenon of *absence*: something not in place for the patient's protection when that structure collapses. The reason for any individual analyst to neglect the patient is here of less interest than avoidance on the part of a profession: a motivated, willed silence. The failure to consider the literal loss of the transference figure, the person the patient has been invited to love (and hate), may reveal, in Freud's language, the "tendency to a counter-transference" in the profession. Winnicott's word "retaliation" carries the formulation further: the failure to consider the matter of the analyst's death may reflect a retaliation more problematic, and potentially more destructive to treatment, than the death itself—an unconscious enactment of the profession's collective frustration or, in a word, hatred. To repeat Winnicott's formulation: "even the actual death of the analyst is not as bad as the development in the analyst of a change of attitude toward retaliation" (1969: 714).

Freud (1893) reportedly liked quoting Charcot. "Theory is good, but it doesn't prevent things from existing" (13, n. 2). It also doesn't prevent things from happening. Both people in the consulting room are real and both can die or be a fool. If the discipline of psychoanalysis locates at its heart an intense, intimate, private relationship with the reliable professional caretaker, shouldn't its theory incorporate the fact of that caretaker's mortality—an ultimate unreliability? In reviewing Schwartz and Silver's collection *Illness in the Analyst* (1990), an early compilation of papers on the subject, Laurel Samuels (1992) writes: "It is a sad commentary that nowhere is reported an example of a therapist fully acknowledging to the patient his/her final illness" (34). She points out that "[e]ven the title of the book omits reference to the distasteful possibility of the therapist's death" (33).

...

Let me pause now to pose a question: Is what I'm saying true? Are patients, in fact, ever abandoned this way? I'll offer two brief examples, one from the discipline's early years, one more recent.

Karl Abraham died suddenly in 1925, following many months of speculation about his delay in resuming his practice. His patient Alix Strachey writes to her husband, James, about the discontinuity: "Yesterday I telephoned … and was, as I expected, told to telephone again on Sunday morning. He *may* possibly, they say, start again on Monday, but they don't sound very convincing. A damned nuisance" (Meisel and Kendrick 1985: 279, italics in original). According to Meisel and Kendrick, Abraham was "steadily growing worse, although the full extent of his illness was as yet unknown even to those closest to him" (290). Further on they note that Abraham's "sudden and premature death (he was only forty-eight) came as a personal and professional shock to the whole psychoanalytic community" (306). It is believed that Abraham died of lung cancer.

Leap ahead eighty years, to 2005, and another patient, Mr. B, tells of his analyst's lung cancer. Unlike Karl Abraham, B's sick analyst returns to work following medical treatment: "Dr. X seems fully recovered," writes B, "back to where he was a few months before he had to stop working. He said the radiation results were much faster than expected—'unprecedented' was the word he used" (private correspondence).

B tells that Dr. X continues to *seem* well, though his condition is in the room, with the oxygen tubing that trails from his face, back beyond his chair and out the interior office door. Dr. X dies unexpectedly, as B experiences it, nine months later and, according to B:

> apparently without having made any arrangements for his patients, as far as I know—or at least without having made any arrangements for me … I was literally left standing on the lawn when I showed up for my session … informed by his wife, through the door, that he was not feeling well and was still in bed. Then when I left a message on his answering machine the following week to confirm my next appointment, she returned the call the next morning to let me know he had passed away the night before. "Oh no, I'm so sorry," was all I could say, repeating it twice more with increasing emotion as I felt the loss, first for him, then for her, then for myself. "Thank you, take good care, and good-bye," she said. And that was that.
>
> (private correspondence)

B's account of this untimely loss is remarkably forgiving and humane toward what is, after all, an abandonment.

It could be argued that every loss is in some sense untimely, but a particular kind of untimely loss is in the fabric of the psychoanalytic engagement, defined by its conceptual framework. Here again therapy is a mirror of real life with its boundaries great and small: people die, the hour ends, termination is a goal. The analyst, as "keeper of the analytic process" (Calef and Weinshel 1980: 279), applies a skill, guided always by his theory, within a carefully structured situation that intends its tilt. But the analyst can apply this keeper's skill only because roles are defined, the activity is disciplined, the relationship is limited, the weekend comes, and termination impends. The mirror as an object is also a bounded as well as polished surface, reflecting in two dimensions what passes before it, within its clearly defined, visible borders.

The therapeutic relationship fosters an intimacy that repeatedly and incrementally *intends* separation—a built-in loss. It could be argued that every ending, even the most unproblematic, involves an untimely loss because, as Bergmann (1997) puts it, "[on] a certain date, every analysis comes to an abrupt end" (137). The ultimate parting is adumbrated in the ritualized ending (or limit) of even the most ordinary therapy hour: a literally, synthetically, "timely" loss recapitulating an event that has not yet happened. Just as "mortal nature" implies far more about the therapist's human limitation than that he can die, the notion of "untimely loss" has larger meaning and may take many forms.

For example, a sick therapist may be untimely lost, though temporarily, if his illness makes him absent, whether for a month or just a day; or, he may be physically present and simultaneously untimely lost if illness makes him distracted and inattentive; to take the reasoning further (and into the future), the analyst who commits an ethical violation may be "untimely lost," profoundly so—even to those patients he has treated ethically, the miscreant doctor is lost retrospectively, less drastically or perhaps less dramatically, yet, in a way, more essentially. The analyst's most ordinary intervention, the act of interpretation, induces loss: the interpretation says "No," prodding the patient to self-observation that promotes differentiation, growth, and the acceptance of limitation with the attendant mourning for what is relinquished. Even the analyst's noncommittal silence or non-intervention constitutes a kind of loss—"untimely" because, just when the patient would like an absolving comment, the doctor becomes orphic or clams up entirely.

In each of these examples of loss, the patient's mourning is not only productive but required. How does he or she successfully, functionally, even gratifyingly, mourn the untimely loss of the partner? What are the potential effects of interruption of process, and of truncated or absent termination? I speak of "termination" here in the technical sense; nothing more absolutely manifests a termination, nothing could be more final and more irrevocable, than a death.

Finally, and of paramount importance, something survives. If the patient is fortunate, the therapy itself may survive, in consciousness and as extended with another analyst, although it is not the same therapy. Or, the patient's loss may be double: he or she may lose both a person and a process, both the therapist and the therapy for which that person was vehicle. The nature of therapeutic treatment itself is double: on one side, a professional function, with necessary clinical principles; on the other, the exertions of a particular soul, necessarily imperfect. The absence of careful provision for the patient, in the sense both of *theoria* and practice, before the collapse of the treatment frame, speaks to a professional denial of Olympian proportions. Only gods need not consider their mortality, and only gods need not grieve.

This truth suggests a further reason for viewing "charismatic analyst" as a contradiction in terms: the analyst may strike a charismatic pose to enact his grievance—unconsciously seeking recompense for whatever he has suffered and, in his role, been denied. Like Freud's (1917) bereaved melancholic, the aggrieved analyst perhaps knows "*whom* he has lost but not *what* he has lost in him" (245). Grandiosity, while it can be charismatic, may be a compensation that prevents or supplants mourning. We need to confront the possibility that an abuse is enacted out of a failure to mourn: to mourn for the loss of the one whose treatment will end, to mourn for each individual practitioner's human limitations, for the fact that the doctor too will eventually die, and to mourn for the limitations of psychoanalysis itself.

In 1912 Freud presented his famous metaphor for the doctor's conduct during psychoanalytic treatment. According to that analogy, the analyst models his behavior on the surgeon "who puts aside all his feelings, even his human sympathy, and concentrates his mental forces on the single aim of performing the operation as skillfully as possible" (Freud 1912c: 115). Implicit in that often-criticized comparison is everything that comes before the actual "cool" surgical procedure—in other words, all that leads up to the mutative and healing work. What precedes any surgery is the careful, meticulous inquiry into the symptom—the analysis of it. As Loewald writes:

> The work of the surgeon does not consist exclusively in the operation itself. There are preoperative and post operative [*sic*] procedures, dressings, dietetic measures, and the like. The same *mutatis mutandis* goes for the researcher in any field. In our zeal to be pure analysts we tend to forget all this.
>
> (1980 [1970]: 298)

Viewed in this light, Freud's analogy is not entirely stark or cold. In that more nuanced analogy, what happens if a heart surgeon dies while performing a delicate operation? The patient is protected by the intervention of another attending surgeon, and a medical team sees the person through to recovery, as is their responsibility. The provision is routine for a surgical patient's protection when the doctor dies but not at all clear for a therapy patient's protection when that doctor dies.

This difference can't be attributed simply to the fact that without help the heart surgery patient will likely die whereas the therapy patient most likely (although not necessarily) will survive. Nor can the difference be attributed to the presence of another doctor during the surgical procedure, while the therapeutic exchange takes place in private. Sometimes offered as rationale, protecting the patient's confidentiality becomes one more form of denial: common sense and humanity dictate that professional responsibility include attention to confidentiality without abandoning the patient. Logically extended, the surgical metaphor assures the patient protection. In actual practice, however, down through the psychoanalytic generations, that protection has often been grossly neglected.

I have emphasized that this implicit mortality is essential to psychoanalytic work. The analyst's imperfection fuels, at the same time as it threatens, every therapeutic engagement. Mortality, in both the positive and negative senses, can be a measure of humanity. Gardner (1983) writes: "And psychoanalysts try mechanically not to be mechanical. They try to show they are human. How can we *show* we are human? Either we are human or we are not" (4). This mordant formulation suggests the difficulty—and the dangers—of a practice that substitutes its own manners for those which culture has evolved over the centuries. I cite it partly as a caution to my own enterprise here: theoretical and practical solutions in this area are not easily fabricated. No human relationship, and no set of manners, can abolish the defects of self-contradiction, awkwardness, or sheer loss. But the customary manners of a profession can, if they rest upon adequate theory, limit and palliate those mortal defects, as is the ultimate purpose of all manners.

The transference is at the core of psychoanalysis and its manners. It intertwines, on one side, the patient's pledge to candor and, on the other, the analyst's commitment to abstinence in benevolent neutrality. It provides, simultaneously, a mirror and a shield. In the story of Medusa and Perseus, the shield *is* a mirror. This fact suggests a triangular configuration. At one point of the triangle is Medusa, the terrifying Gorgon with the snaky locks. At the second point is Perseus, the hero who slays the monster. At the third point of my imagined triangle is the vehicle, or means, by which Perseus accomplishes the feat: his polished, reflective shield.

Perseus holds up that bright shield and mirror in which the image of the Gorgon is reflected, enabling him to kill her without looking directly at her, which would turn him to stone. In that perfect, protective surface, the defect, or ugliness, is visible but no longer fatal or immobilizing. *Held* in the shield—it could be called an "enchanted glass"—is the transference. Safe-kept by the analyst, the process is a clear mirror, and a reliable shield, and—what's more—the hero is clearly the patient.

Notes

1   This text originally appeared, in a slightly different form, as part of "Physic Himself Must Fade," *American Imago*, 69(1) (2012): 29–56. Reprinted with permission.

2   It is not within the scope of this chapter to elaborate upon efforts to address the subject more openly. For one example, Amy Morrison (1990) writes movingly about her work with patients over the ten years of her illness; Feinsilver (1998) and Traesdal (2005) also provide impressive examples.

Chapter 2

The Potion[1]

> [A]s all is mortal in nature, so is all nature in love mortal in folly.
> —Touchstone, *As You Like It*, II, 4

The idealized image of a mirror that is also a shield fails to include other, more unstable and conflictual aspects of the psychoanalytic situation—an extraordinary arrangement where two people talk in a way that, in Freud's (1915a) words, has no parallel: "The course the analyst must pursue," he writes, "is one for which there is no model in real life" (166). And though the image of a reflective and containing shield has its merits, the arrangement also invites—intends to invite—(here's another, different image) a conflagration.

"No model in real life"—that is an astonishing assertion. What is Freud talking about? If there is no model for this artifice-that-is-not-artificial, what form does it take? What dangers does it carry? What image or formulation is adequate to those incendiary dangers? Richard Roud (1980) wrote of Jean Renoir's masterwork, *The Rules of the Game*, that "if France were destroyed tomorrow and nothing remained but this film, the whole country and its civilization could be reconstructed from it" (841).

And what about the "talking cure"?

Imagine the entire psychoanalytic literature is destroyed tomorrow. Psychoanalysis vanishes, but you can bury a time capsule to be dug up after a few hundred years. Into that capsule you can put a few papers—a handful of short works people of the future might use to reconstruct psychoanalysis: as mirror, as shield, and also as something more ambiguous, even messy.

Over time, I've added or removed papers from my own imaginary capsule. But certain things are always there—for example, Hans Loewald's paper on therapeutic action (1960), Paula Heimann's "On

Counter-Transference" (1950), Winnicott's "The Use of an Object" (1969). Sometimes I include Brian Bird's "Notes on Transference" (1972), Macalpine's "The Development of Transference" (1950), a paper by Melanie Klein, John Klauber, or André Green. It's always useful to argue why a particular essay is indispensable to reconstructing psychoanalysis.

For me, as maybe not for some, Freud always takes up a lot of room in the capsule, with two of his briefest papers competing for first and second place: "Remembering, Repeating and Working-Through" (1914) and "Observations on Transference-Love" (1915). In these two closely linked short pieces (barely twenty pages in all)—rich, maddening, impossible to exhaust—in these two essays, I find the foundation.

But if I have to choose, "Observations on Transference-Love" reigns alone at the top of the list. It's the quintessential document—defining the clinical setup, charting its dangers, providing ethical precepts for guiding treatment, and, perhaps above all, in the context of those ethical questions, confronting the immense power and necessary strangeness of the transference: that form of love, or attachment, a shield and a—a volatile *something*—that fuels the process and can burst into flame. Is it a flammable potion? A magic formula?

When I first read the essay many years ago as a graduate student, it confused me with its turnabouts; annoyed me with its tone about women; bemused me with its wit and off-color comedy—I think of the demeaning description of "women of elemental passionateness who … are accessible only to 'the logic of soup, with dumplings for arguments'" (Freud 1915a: 166–167), and of the sexualized joke about dogs and sausages Freud invokes to capture the forbidden in the analytic doctor's "line of action":

> For the doctor, ethical motives unite with the technical ones to restrain him from giving the patient his love … He must not stage the scene of a dog-race in which the prize was to be a garland of sausages but which some humorist spoilt by throwing a single sausage on the track. The result was, of course, that the dogs threw themselves upon it and forgot all about the race and about the garland that was luring them to victory in the far distance.
>
> (Freud 1915a: 169)

In the effort to chart how the analyst must behave "not to come to grief" over the erotic transference, Freud (1915a) takes a curious tone with this joke (163). Is he condescending? Does he smirk, revealing his discomfort? Nevertheless, in its conversational manner, and its remarkable twists and turns, "Observations on Transference-Love" mesmerized me. Not only does the essay lay down technical principles and ethical precepts, but it teaches us that they are the same thing.

This idea, that for the analyst the ethical and the technical are inseparable, will be a central point of my effort to examine the force—we call it the transference—that propels the healing process. Though written a hundred years ago, and cast as instructions for the beginner, Freud's paper is more relevant today, in my view, amid the welter of accumulated orthodoxies and refinements and revisions.

"Observations on Transference-Love" is Freud's (1915a) methodical argument for what he calls the "fundamental principle of the treatment being carried out in abstinence" (165)—the analyst says, "No," tacitly setting up the forbidden: an absolute embedded in the restrictions of the setting. With abstinence comes the closely associated though distinct notion of neutrality, the former referring to the analyst's behavior (he does not yield to the patient's invitation), the latter to the analyst's attitude, a benevolent receptivity not to be confused with coldness, or not caring. Freud never meant by these often-caricatured terms "the deprivation of everything that the patient desires" (165); nor did he think the human analyst "proof against every temptation" (166). With these two concepts, abstinence and neutrality, plus the essential third element—the patient's requirement to say everything, the pledge to candor—with these three structuring principles, Freud gives us psychoanalytic treatment. Everything follows in a complex way from that basis: principles that are spacious ideals, and never intended as tidy rules.

Abstinence, neutrality, and candor, then, structure the psychoanalytic situation. Two people, patient and analyst, meet privately and regularly; they don't touch—implicitly proscribing sexual activity, which becomes taboo (incestuous); and the patient freely speaks his or her desire to the analyst, who listens with a benign receptivity, not to judge but to understand, and to offer back that understanding—a reciprocal offering called "interpretation." I've identified this as a combustible arrangement. The image of fire is Freud's (1915a) own—he speaks of "highly explosive forces" unleashed by the transference, whereby "a woman patient shows by unmistakable indications, or openly declares, that she has fallen in love, as any other mortal woman might, with the doctor who is analyzing her"

(159). Freud's phrase, "as any other mortal woman might," speaks to the induced headiness of the situation, and captures a tender side as well: the woman is not immortal, not out of nature, she's an ordinary human being, she's in love, and demands that her love be returned.

Freud (1915a) joins the simile of combustion to another figurative element—theatrical performance: "There is a complete change of scene; it is as though some piece of make-believe had been stopped by the sudden irruption of reality—as when, for instance, a cry of fire is raised during a theatrical performance" (162). This alarming "irruption of reality" in the psychoanalytic theater is the woman patient's "passionate demand for love," a fiery desire evoked in the developing transference. Something comparable to the power of theater art is interrupted by a different kind of power, more like the physical threats of fire and crowd panic. Unlike the theater, however, the analytic stage invites real risk, even *requires* it; and the psychoanalyst knows that he "needs to proceed with as much caution and conscientiousness as a chemist" (Freud 1915a: 170).

But the fire alarm is in the script. The abstinent analyst performs as a deliberately incendiary human lure in a process focusing and magnifying the patient's love cravings. Freud (1915a) is clear that anything interfering with "the continuation of the treatment may be an expression of resistance," and he has no doubt, in this instance, that the woman's passionate intensity is "the work of resistance" (162)—Freud's term for those unconscious forces in the patient interfering with remembering, and manifesting her reciprocal "No." Suddenly, the analyst is center stage in a "real" life drama; the patient seems "swallowed up in her love" and wants it returned—her docility, her intelligence, her insight are gone; memory is replaced by alarming passion and the treatment comes to a halt. In this way the resistance makes use of the woman's love, "acting as an agent provocateur" (163), intensifying her passion in order to hinder the treatment.

Or so it seems. But Freud (1915a) tells us that appearances are deceptive. Though the woman's "falling in love in the transference" (162) might at first look disadvantageous, the same agent provocateur that threatens the scene also animates the treatment, dramatizing the patient's inexpressible (because unconscious) difficulty. The link to "Remembering, Repeating and Working-Through," written one year earlier, is apparent.

As Max Hernandez (1993) concisely puts this transference/resistance paradox, "Love is the motor of the analytic cure as well as the main obstacle to it" (98). Freud, having written eight times in the essay's first pages simply that the woman "falls in love" with the doctor, here the crucial ninth time deftly adds "in the transference," explicitly qualifying his subject. Is the temperature building as he elaborates on this induced passion? One could say the terms "transference" and "resistance," though necessary to structure the setting and to guide the analyst's thinking, serve also to deflect from the strangeness of what the analyst sets in motion: Freud is perhaps muffling the doctor's own activity as agent provocateur—someone who offers himself as a hook to snare desire.

Freud's hypothetical patient serves as an extreme instance of transference intensity. However, he acknowledges the narrowness of his focus, noting in a footnote the "less tender feelings" that can manifest in the transference (1915a: 161, n. 1). How strange are the analytic form and function? Masud Khan elaborates Freud's achievement in structuring a ritual scene:

> [H]ow ingeniously Freud had ritualistically established taboos that made incest and parricide in this very exclusive human community of two persons impossible. The basic taboos are: of motility (lying on the couch), and of sight and touch (the ego functions that normally intensify excitement most readily). To these taboos Freud had adjoined a revolutionary transgression: he invited and facilitated the patient to express his incestuous and parricidal wishes through the *Word*. Thus the taboos create that area of illusion where language explores and expresses the wish-system. Without this illusion language would yield merely humiliation and remorse.
>
> (1973: 233)

Khan here couples taboo with "revolutionary transgression," filling out, perhaps, the meaning of Freud's astonishing "no model." In "Observations on Transference-Love" Freud struggles to measure the audacity of the analyst's activity: taboo and transgression. Psychoanalysis creates a "no, you may not" coupled with a "yes, you must"—don't move, don't look, don't touch, but speak the words that expressively reflect the desire.

Like a stage play, the artifice of the psychoanalytic process, as Freud describes it, contains the transgressive by ritualizing it. "Observations on Transference-Love" refers explicitly to magic rituals. Responding to the patient's erotic transference by urging that it be renounced or suppressed, Freud (1915a) writes, "would be just as though, after summoning up a spirit from the underworld by cunning spells, one were to send him down again without having asked him a single question" (164). Neither rejecting the love nor responding to it—the course for which "there is no model in real life"—the analyst instead treats it as unreal. In the analyst's not acting on the love, coupled with the expectation that the patient speak it, the patient's longing persists and intensifies.

The "cunning spells" or magic potions have had unintended consequences. As in Freud's own time, "boundary violation" (the discipline's current euphemism) remains embarrassingly common. Usually the clinician is a man, often professionally distinguished, with years of experience, and the patient a younger woman. Freud (1915a) treats the analyst who succumbs to this pattern with a dry, corrective irony: "[the analyst] must recognize that the patient's falling in love is induced by the analytic situation and is not to be attributed to the charms of his own person; so that he has no grounds whatever for being proud of such a 'conquest', as it would be called outside analysis" (160–161). In other words, the analytic doctor must not confuse the enchantment of the situation with "the charms of his own person."

Can erotic feelings be so delusory, ductile, nearly arbitrary, induced by a construct? The Shakespeare scholar Stephen Greenblatt describes the fairies' "love juice" in *A Midsummer Night's Dream*:

> Desires in *A Midsummer Night's Dream* are intense, irrational and alarmingly mobile. This mobility, the speed with which desire can be detached from one object and attached to a different object, does not diminish the exigency of the passion, for the lovers are convinced at every moment that their choices are irrefutably rational and irresistibly compelling. … The emblem, as well as agent, of a dangerously mobile desire is the fairies' love juice. No human being in the play experiences a purely abstract, objectless desire; when you desire, you desire someone. But the love juice is the distilled essence of erotic mobility itself, and it is appropriately in the power of the fairies.
>
> (1997: 810)

The two people in the consulting room, analyst and patient, are merely talking, but in a way that invites the mobility of desire, with an intensity like the stage-woods of Midsummer Eve. The psychoanalytic process devises that love juice, channels it, and distributes it for a special use. The fairies' potion is in us all, with its insistent, dizzying, fluent power. Easy here to see the likeness to Freud's "cathexis," which, as Paula Heimann (1956) describes it, "presupposes the existence of a mobile energy, derived from the instinctual reservoir, which can be moved from one place to another, from the subject to an object, from one object to others" (303). In *A Midsummer Night's Dream*, do the characters truly love each other? Or is it the potion?

In the analytic situation, however, the potion—Greenblatt's "distilled essence of erotic mobility itself"—is not in the power of a magical creature in a theatrical drama. It's in the power of the human analyst on the tilted, and private, analytic stage. The analyst plays with fire! What brings about such madness? Historically, a standard explanation of the "irruption of fire" attributes the patient's falling in love to the arrangement itself—the rules, the frame, the analyst's technical procedures—tending to leave the person of the analyst out of it. He (or she) doesn't make it happen, it's the setting.

On such a tidy but limited understanding, the situation itself, supposedly, entices, while the analyst is merely the analyst, doing analysis: an innocent, more like a steward or dull chaperone than a breathing human lure for someone's love cravings. And in a sense this is true: the analyst's most essential and difficult task is to restore the virtuality of the transference—Freud's (1914b) "intermediate region between illness and real life" (154) where healing takes place—and through his interpretive understanding to get things back up onto the play stage. In that sense, the interpreting analyst is both reliable shepherd and guide. In finding words to convey his understanding of the sources of the patient's suffering, he (or she) is guardian of the treatment.

But why do I call this way of understanding limited? Because it skirts the issue. To assign the "seduction" merely to the situation is self-justifying, a way of deflecting, even disavowing, the real—and in a sense uncanny?—discomfort and danger inherent in the analyst's position. Sidney Tarachow (1963) astutely observed some fifty years ago that "object hunger is as much a problem of the therapist as it is the patient's" (17); both people have "a basic urge to mutual acting out," a human need and wish for a real object (Tarachow 1962: 380). The analyst's act that transforms the real into an *as-if* is interpretation: "The imposition of this barrier [to reality] creates a therapeutic task for both patient and therapist" (380), countering the inevitable temptations to come closer together. Hans Loewald's (1971) idea is similar, describing the analyst's task as a "persistent renunciation of involvement, a constant activity of uninvolving which tends to impel the patient to understand himself in his involvement" (63).

The analyst's interpretation, then, is another form of "No, we may not," the same proscription that ignites desire, for both people. As Friedman (1991) puts it, "in the back of his mind the analyst always knew … that he could not divorce himself from his procedures. He knew that it was he (or she) … who enticed and endangered the patient" (94). The "no" of the setting's restrictions stirs up the "yes" of "I want," thus directly implicating the analyst in the combustion. Fidias Cesio (1993) is helpfully blunt: "In the very act of enunciating the setting as a 'prohibition' of direct sexual activity, the analyst is *the protagonist of incest* but, as Freud says, he is so with due 'considerations of analytic technique', that is, *as a technical device …*" (139, emphasis added). With that extraordinary coupling—"the protagonist of incest … as a technical device"—psychoanalytic treatment takes its strange shape.

Freud struggles with precisely this discomfort and danger in "Observations on Transference-Love." In ending, he returns to fire, and the essay concludes, to my ear, with bravado:

> But to believe that the psychoneuroses are to be conquered by operating with harmless little remedies is grossly to under-estimate those disorders both as to their origin and their practical importance. No; in medical practice there will always be room for the '*ferrum*' and the '*ignis*' side by side with the '*medicina*'; and in the same way we shall never be able to do without a strictly regular, undiluted psycho-analysis which is not afraid to handle the most dangerous mental impulses and to obtain mastery over them for the benefit of the patient.
>
> (Freud 1915a: 171)

Ferrum, ignis, and *medicina*. There *are* "highly explosive forces" in the room, there's chemistry, and "chemistry" indicates mutual attraction. Patient and analyst are two people, not one person tended by an articulate robot.

Three years earlier, in the remarkable closing passage of "The Dynamics of Transference," Freud (1912a) makes vivid the inevitable heat and struggle—indeed, the battle—between two people, patient and analyst, the forces alive in the room:

> But it should not be forgotten that it is precisely [transference phenomena] that do us the inestimable service of making the patient's hidden and forgotten erotic impulses immediate and manifest. For

when all is said and done, it is impossible to destroy anyone *in absentia* or *in effigie*.

(Freud 1912a: 108)

I agree with those who view the psychoanalytic situation as a structured invitation to fall in love, a form of arrested or circumscribed seduction, courting the transgressive. To seduce, from the Latin *seducere*, is to lead away. "Desire, in human sexuality, is always transgression; and being something that is never completely fulfilled, its object cannot ever offer full satisfaction" (Kohon 1984: 77). Chetrit-Vatine (2014) terms the asymmetrical analytic engagement an "ethical seduction," that oxymoron capturing the analyst's paradoxical position as well as responsibility. As a human medium, the analyst's character is always being tested, as he (or she) resists the enticements and provocations not only of the transference—a psychological seduction, leading away, with the aim to bring back—but of the actual real-life, two-person engagement through which the "bringing-back" unfolds.

Here are two crucial, interrelated ideas: first, the analyst's moral integrity is a technical requirement as well as the patient's ultimate safeguard. Ida Macalpine (1950), echoing Freud, understood this point mid-century, locating "form" in the analyst's moral integrity: "it is a technical device and not a moral precept" (527). And second, in a profound paradox, *abstinence* is *alluring*—the principle of abstinence protects but, by design, also heats the treatment crucible. That paradox captures the analyst's inevitable necessary discomfort. In his remarkable 1912 paper, "On the Universal Tendency to Debasement in the Sphere of Love," from the same period as *Papers on Technique*, Freud writes:

It can be easily shown that the psychical value of erotic needs is reduced as soon as their satisfaction becomes easy. An obstacle is required in order to heighten libido; and where natural resistances to satisfaction have not been sufficient men have at all times erected conventional ones.

(1912b: 187)

The analyst, one could say, intentionally erects such an obstacle, though "conventional" would apply only within the strange ritual form. Questions follow. Outside the form, in "ordinary" life, might the analyst's abstinent conduct be located on a continuum that includes, at its far end, the sadistic (if not the perverse)? Is the membrane that separates the two—the manners of ordinary life and of the clinical realm—more porous than that? However one answers, it seems reasonable that, when Freud addresses this "universal" predisposition, he plants (though perhaps not consciously) a significant warning: the "tendency to debasement" hovers in the treatment room.

"The aim of the analyst," writes Forrester (1990), "is always double: to entice or attract, and then to decline and evade, to defer and delay" (84). In more colloquial language, the analyst's technical stance, structurally, includes elements of a tease, "the queasy uncertainty of [a] shifting come-on" (Friedman 2005: 426). Freud recognized early, in *Studies on Hysteria*, writes Friedman (1997), "that [the analyst] was doing something forbidden to physicians; he was deliberately courting a personal, affective intimacy." Friedman (1997) quotes Freud: patients "put themselves in the doctor's hands and place their confidence in him—a step which in other situations is only taken voluntarily and never at the doctor's request (Breuer and Freud [1895], p. 266)" (25).

To this volatile mix we can add what Freud, in the same early text, calls the "special solicitude inherent in the treatment" (Breuer and Freud 1895: 302)—a focused attention that builds rapport (transformed into tidier psychoanalytic terms, the "unobjectionable positive transference") but, at the same time, joined with the analyst's abstinence, courts the erotic transference. "In not a few cases," writes Freud:

> especially with women and where it is a question of elucidating erotic trains of thought, the patient's co-operation becomes a personal sacrifice, which must be compensated by some substitute for love. The trouble taken by the physician and his friendliness have to suffice for such a substitute.
>
> (Breuer and Freud 1895: 301)

The analyst, that is, compensates the patient for her sacrifice—her "cooperation" in speaking her desire—by a "substitute": his own effort and his friendly attention. It hardly sounds, on the face of it, like a fair or reasonable deal.

What kind of caring *is* this? What are its ingredients? Moreover, what will the patient—besotted by the potion—make of what's offered? All of this teasing, all this illusion and uncertainty, this courting and playing with mysteries, with inexplicable and semi-explicable meanings. Is the process natural? Unseemly? Is it trickery? A ruse? As I write these sentences, I hear the Platters singing Jerome Kern and Otto Harbach's "Smoke Gets in Your Eyes," in 1958:

> They said some day you'll find
>> All who love are blind
>> When your heart's on fire
>> You must realize
>> Smoke gets in your eyes.

How does this induced blindness lead to transformed vision?

I want to be clear: I'm not saying the situation is corrupt but that it is corruptible, perhaps inherently so (though not so dangerously corruptible as, say, a celibate priesthood). "Corruption" suggests something dishonest, and covert. At the very least, the enterprise is full of paradoxes and contradictions: the situation is real, it's unreal; it's staged, it's real life; it's personal, it's impersonal; it's personal, it's theoretical; it's an artifice, it's not artificial; it starts with "no," it stirs up "yes"; it provides safeties, these safeties heat things up; it frustrates, it relaxes; it forbids, it permits; if it succeeds, it disappoints (try saying that about your orthopedic surgery); "psycho-analytic treatment is founded on truthfulness" (Freud 1915a: 164) but begins with a seduction; it's founded on truthfulness but self-deception is fundamental to being human—no concept is more psychoanalytic than this last.

What will prepare the analyst for such an "impossible profession"?

This device, or ritual, that has "no model" can be justified only if it provides an avenue to a region of extraordinary complexity—the unconscious mind—otherwise inaccessible, and potentially the source of restorative insight, and healing.

Writing about the analyst's own analysis in "Analysis Terminable and Interminable," Freud (1937) says (with striking simplicity) that the analyst's analysis "has accomplished its purpose if it gives the learner a firm conviction of the existence of the unconscious, if it enables him, when repressed material emerges, to perceive in himself things which would otherwise be *incredible* to him ..." (248, emphasis added). Can one *believe* it? What gives firm conviction, and credibility, to the "incredible"? The complexities of psychic life are so manifold, the interaction between conscious and unconscious mind so mysterious and infinitely complex, that one can almost doubt what we take as evidence. Dreaming, for example, that rich form of narrative produced in sleep. Is it chance? Neurons firing? Magic? The potion? Beyond "the existence of the unconscious," what is its nature, in general and in particular?

Early in my analysis I had this dream: the dreamer finds herself at a crossroads marked by signs on a mountain path high on a slope above the sea. The scene is cartoonish, nothing looks quite real. One marker points to a "high road," a second to a "low road." The dreamer takes the high road but becomes stuck midway, sandwiched by two more arrow-shaped signs planted in the middle of the path. These enormous signs blocking her way point in opposite directions: one arrow reads in bold capital letters LOUGON, the other reads LONDON. Far below this mountain is the ocean; it may be labeled MER. The dreamer seems to know that these signs allude to two previous lost therapists—"Lou" in LOUGON is the beloved uncle called to mind by a first therapist, now dead, and LONDON alludes to a second therapist's accent. Paralyzed, unable to move in either direction, the dreamer watches, immobilized. Then two large white birds lift away off the side of the slope and fly out over the water together. The feeling that accompanies their flight is suffused with relief.

On waking, I review the dream in my mind's eye, taking in its cartoonish character. I see the bold signs, so striking in the dream, and play with the letters, a symmetry that was clear even while dreaming: the same number of letters in each sign; both destinations begin with "L" and end with "N." And then, a couple of seaward-bound water birds emerge from the signs, formed by the first two and last two letters in each— two "loons." The play on "loons" (birdbrains, loonies, divers, laughers, lovebirds, doves—are loons even *white*?) is pleasing for the delighted yet incredulous beginning analysand, growing giddy with the potion, and further inebriated by the associative process itself. The dreamer is in love with her own production, as if to say: "Look what I made, and now look what I can say about it!"

And there is plenty to say about the dream, but I'll focus on only one further element, possibly the ingredient hardest for me to believe, as well as the most self-intoxicating: in the dream there is an anagram. Finding (and freeing) the loons requires removing the two middle letters from each sign, leaving "UG" from one, "ND" from the other. Just a messy clot of letters—until, unscrambling them, I make DUNG. Who would *believe* that? Certainly, *I* had trouble believing it. Is it chance? Neurons firing randomly? Magic? Is it a kind of quasi-authorial overexcitement—or just crap? (Now I hear Mel Brooks' psychiatrist Dr. Thorndyke in *High Anxiety* asking an audience at a psychiatric conference, is the topic "number one," or "cocky-doody"?)

What makes it possible for the dreamer (any dreamer, any therapy patient) to embark? Among many things, my dream is about a desired return to the mother—*la mère*—and to dream it required the risk of trusting someone else—*as if* it were an intense love relation: a falling in love "in the transference." On the crucial subject of trust, Freud is remarkably clear:

> The more plainly the analyst lets it be seen that he is proof against every temptation, the more readily will he be able to extract from the situation its analytic content. The patient … will then feel safe enough to allow all her preconditions for loving, … all the detailed characteristics of her state of being in love, to come to light …
>
> (1915a: 166)

The ethical and technical unite. They are not separable.

The "high road" in my dream is perhaps the idealization of early transference love, a form of denial, and an escape—in Freud's vocabulary, "resistance"—and the twin birds, freed of the dirty waste, fly away together over the ocean. To put it another way, the dream perhaps tells the dreamer: "Cut the crap and get to work." The analysis has begun, and the flight (and I do mean "flight" in both senses, elevation and retreat), the flight will be long.

Does this brief chemical analysis of a dramatic scene, conjured in sleep and stirred by the potion, reveal something that would otherwise seem "incredible"? Does it give Freud's learner "a firm conviction of the existence of the unconscious"? And what about the low road? I'll return to those dream-matters in a minute.

As the reader may well detect, there is a bone I'm worrying. This is powerful material the analyst is handling: chemicals, combustibles, "mental impulses" to extract and examine, having called them up from the underworld "in the transference." What are the risks attendant upon a setup that so intensely pulls for passions, deliberately heats up desires, yet so stringently requires renunciation, for both people? The analyst is not "really" a seducer, though he is seductive—*actual* seduction, we all know (and perhaps, turning a blind eye, too easily take for granted), must not be the outcome. But the ritualized arrangement positions him precariously. The situation puts exquisite pressure on certain human traits: an ordinary person in a vulnerable position.

The structured invitation for the patient to fall in love presents complex risks, with many temptations embedded in the power of the transference: the most troubling of these, perhaps, the invitation for the analyst, the purveyor of illusion, in his (or her) human capacity for self-deception, and grandiosity, to believe he inhabits an enchanted kingdom, like Shakespeare's fairies, magical in his powers. The analyst, drunk on the love juice, may feel justified, thrilled by "the charms of his own person" and their effect—he believes he is himself a bit magical, charismatic.

Freud's tone about this ever-present danger in "Observations on Transference-Love" recalls *A Midsummer Night's Dream*. The cool, smiling irony of Freud's "not to be attributed to the charms of his own person" mocks the notion of charisma. Self-deluding, the idea of a personal charisma beyond the structural is also, as a matter of theory, redundant. As a moral or ethical matter, it is radically defective: a charismatic analyst, within the clinical setting, is a massively destructive contradiction in terms. *It punishes trust.* The patient's love is a construct provoked by the analytic situation, and it is the responsibility of the analyst, having set the process in motion, to limit and protect it.

In Shakespeare's play, Bottom, the loquacious clown, becomes an ass-headed man who by magic potion becomes adored by the enchanted fairy queen Titania. For her, Bottom becomes charismatic. The boastful, ambitious Bottom himself, with his ass's ears, believes he *is* charismatic. In Freud's terms, Bottom believes in "the charms of his own person."

But while Freud says, wisely enough, that it's not the analyst's own charms that enrapture the patient, perhaps in another sense that is exactly what happens. In a well-conducted analysis, guided by the analyst's abstinence and neutrality, the transference *is* a kind of enchantment, transitory and functional. As Max Hernandez writes:

> Once an analysis is over—one hesitates to say finished—the memory that the analyst or the analysand has of it, and especially the written account of it, is but a pale reflection of what happened during the analysis to either of them or between them. All one knows is that it occurred once upon a time.
>
> (Hernandez 1993, 101)

It occurred once upon a time but the enchantment can still be called up. One way it's called up is in dreams. I believe this can be true for any analysand (or, in a sense, for anyone). Perhaps it's even an element in why one writes. The enchantment is called up in trying to write an essay like this one. "Writing was in its origin the voice of an absent person," writes Freud (1930), "and the dwelling-house was a substitute for the mother's womb, the first lodging, for which in all likelihood man still longs, and in which he was safe and felt at ease" (91). Now I'll return to my dream about the signposts, the mountain, the birds, and returning to the mother.

It was dreamed many years ago, and the analysis has ended— "terminated," in our bizarre lingo. (Talk about skirting tender affect!) "Whatever termination is," writes Gabbard (2009), "it is certainly not the end. Analysands continue to try to work through the loss of the analyst in fantasy, in dreams, and in other relationships" (591). Incorporating the dream into this essay, I found a new element that I had never thought much about before, though I've talked about the dream many times. What about the "low road"? The dreamer will, eventually, have to choose the "low road"—which requires integration, acceptance of imperfection, a letting go, if you like, of an omnipotent denial: a process of mourning (in Freud's language, "working-through"). In the return to the mountain from flight over the ocean, the dreamer now takes the "low road"—and here came the new thought—and now the letters in the anagram can go back where they were, LOUGON (Lou*gone*), LONDON (Lon*done*). But the signs, in their original form, no longer need block the dreamer's path: limitation, with the attendant disappointment, is accepted (returning to the vernacular, they can keep their shit, and the dreamer perhaps more easily tolerates her own). And the birds can separate, marking the end.

If that sounds too tidy, you didn't hear me say the process is ever complete. It's never finished, and then we die. Truisms. Maybe the fact of the final limitation—mortality—is why we strive in the first place. That's not a new idea either. But the awareness of, and rebellion against, mortality—that ultimate blow to our narcissism, our wish for omnipotence—has some relation to love in the analytic setting. Psychoanalysis is a powerful instrument with an enormous potential to help, that helpfulness conjoined with potential to harm, sometimes grievously. What kind of caring is it? What words to capture it?

I have called the therapeutic offering a "mortal gift." It would be located at one end of an imagined continuum that includes the transference enchantment that is the vehicle for healing (Freud's "intermediate region," the area of illusion). I don't object to calling it a mature love, or, if you prefer a little more distance, call it analytic love. Loewald (1980 [1960]) is among those not shy of the word: the analyst's stance, he writes, "requires an objectivity and neutrality the essence of which is love and respect for the individual and for individual development" (229). Writing of the child's first love, Anna Freud is characteristically direct: "The ability to love—like other human faculties—has to be learned and practiced" (Freud and Burlingham 1943: 191). Perhaps the philosopher and mystic Simone Weil (1963) succinctly captures that ability to love, in its maturing, when she writes: "Belief in the existence of other human beings as such is *love*" (56, emphasis in original).

If terms like these, however imperfect, approximate the nature of the analyst's disciplined caring, or love, there is also the matter of the analyst's hate—on my imagined continuum of "caring," located at the other end from the "mortal gift." The problem I'm poking at throughout: the analyst's narcissism in this combustible arrangement, and our discipline's century-long effort to address it. In "Observations on Transference Love," which I have termed the quintessential document, Freud grapples with just that issue. We witness his struggle to find adequate terms for the forces inevitably stirred in the clinical interaction. The power of the potion, as devised in the psychoanalytic situation, heightens the analyst's vulnerability to forgetting himself. How to proceed safely? How to manage the excitement of looking at the forbidden—the analyst's "ineluctably conflictual task"? (Levine 2003: 209; Blum 1981). How to keep the solution balanced, the concentration right? In 1915 Freud was concerned about this, and the situation the paper addresses haunts the profession to this day.

The extensive contemporary literature on boundary violations examines these matters in considerable depth but at the same time deflects and clouds thinking: like the transference process itself, a simultaneous opening up and covering over. When the analyst has sex with a patient, that's ethical misconduct. Few would disagree. But is such exploitation adequately captured by the term "boundary violation"? The term boundary suggests a border, evoking a neatly defined separateness. In baseball, the foul line is marked and the umpire's ruling (more or less) precise.

In contrast, whatever separates the two people in the consulting room is not clear in the same static, linear way but instead is necessarily tense, or kinetic: more like two forces at the line of scrimmage. If our vocabulary doesn't take that built-in aggression into account, it's euphemistic, substituting an inoffensive or soft term for a truer one—a form of evasion. To put the problem in quasi-legal language, the term "boundary" evokes the wrong kind of malfeasance because what happens in the clinical exchange involves more than property lines. It is a fiduciary matter. Violating a "boundary" suggests you've infringed on someone's property line, when in fact the analyst's sexual misconduct is less like crossing lines than it is like an off-sides violation, or like fraud—or, in its most extreme form, like rape.

It could be argued that the current vocabulary of "enactment" attempts better to account for the kinetic, and there is a logic to that idea. But the problematic nature of that quasi-scientific terminology, which in my view is also euphemistic, and evasive, entails what Orgel (1997) refers to as "invoking or constructing theories that rationalize yielding to internal and external 'necessities,' that relieve the analyst of the demands and frustrations of being the protector of the patient's individuality and potential autonomy by maintaining reasonable abstinence and neutrality" (58). Might one view enactment theory, if taken too far, as an invitation to accept, rather than counter (as Tarachow sharply counters it, with the analyst's transforming act of interpretation) the merely human need and wish for a real object, the "basic urge to mutual acting out"? (Tarachow 1962: 380). Where one vocabulary diminishes malfeasance, the other neutralizes it, making the potion more like a bromide—a simple chemical reaction, reductive in comparison to the reality.

The potion. Is it medicinal? Magic? Poisonous? The liquid is powerful, it's thrilling, it's dangerous, it's essential, it's in us all. In the transference, as well as in life, people can fall in love for many reasons—including to fill an internal absence, to manage loneliness, or to avoid something—as Freud points out with the essential concepts of transference and resistance. Is there an antidote, a "potion-diluter," when it's the analyst who is vulnerable and falls in love with the patient "in the countertransference"? Is this truly love? Who's to say? If the analyst acts on that "love," do we still call it love? Is it closer to aggression? Is it more like Winnicott's countertransference hate (1949)? Or, to borrow Stoller's language (1975), is it an "erotic form of hatred"? Anna Freud, in related terms, elaborates on the "ability" to love: "The opposite of this ability to love," she writes, "is not hate but egoism," or self-love (Freud and Burlingham 1943: 191).

I'll end as I began, and offer another image in the hope of capturing an aspect of the complex, endlessly puzzling psychoanalytic situation.

In the story of Orpheus, as told by Bulfinch (1964), the great musician plays and sings to such perfection that he entrances everything—his fellow mortals, the wild beasts, "nay, the very trees and rocks were sensible to the charm" of his music (134). One day his beautiful wife Eurydice, while fleeing a shepherd's advances, "trod on a snake in the grass, was bitten in the foot, and died." Grief-stricken, Orpheus follows her to the underworld, where he implores the deities, in song, to let her return to life with him:

> As he sang these tender strains, the very ghosts shed tears. Tantalus, in spite of his thirst, stopped for a moment his efforts for water, Ixion's wheel stood still, the vulture ceased to tear the giant's liver … and Sisyphus sat on his rock to listen. Then for the first time, it is said, the cheeks of the Furies were wet with tears.
>
> (Bulfinch 1964: 134)

Pluto too finally gives way and permits Orpheus to take Eurydice back with him, but on one condition: "that he should not turn around to look at her till they should have reached the upper air." We all know what happens. Orpheus leads, his wife follows, and as they near the upper world: "Orpheus, in a moment of forgetfulness, to assure himself that she was still following, cast a glance behind him, when instantly she was borne away" (1964: 134).

Orpheus thoughtlessly glances back, Bulfinch writes, "in a moment of forgetfulness." How do we understand a "moment of forgetfulness"? Does the moment contain the forbidden? In the simple turning of his body and the directing of his sight, Orpheus breaches the taboo—a failure to resist the excitement of looking. And the beloved Eurydice dies for the second time.

Note

1 This text originally appeared, in a slightly different version, in *Journal of the American Psychoanalytic Association* 62 (2014): 455–474. Reprinted with permission.

Chapter 3

The Olympian Delusion[1]

Let us stop to ponder the magnitude of Freud's discovery. For centuries men and women have searched for mandrake roots and other substances from which a love potion could be brewed. And then a Jewish Viennese physician uncovered love's secret. There is indeed a way in which one human being can make another fall in love, and the prescription is remarkably simple.

—Martin Bergmann (1986: 30)

Nothing takes place between them except that they talk to each other.
—Sigmund Freud (1926: 187)

This is an essay on an unpleasant subject: a subject so painful that some within the discipline of psychoanalysis wince and turn away from it—the sexual exploitation of patients. The psychoanalytic situation is an audacious endeavor that purposely courts risk: for a time placing one human being *as if* at the center of another's emotional life. In that power-imbalanced relationship, behind closed doors, what is the patient's protection?

Lawrence Friedman (2008a) says the following about Freud's *Papers on Technique*, six essays written between 1911 and 1915: "*Papers on Technique* floats the buoys that mark out psychoanalysis from other human relationships. You can argue about whether to steer this way or that around those markers, but without them you have nothing but open sea" (1032). In these pages, I try to consider what the buoys mean, and the perils they aim to mark. In my view, Freud's most fundamental "buoy" is the principle of abstinence. I am concerned in this chapter with abstinence and integrity, and the shoals and depths that endanger them. I hope to raise more questions than I answer.

The matter is not merely theoretical. In my home city of Boston the psychoanalytic community lost three senior analysts to disgrace in a span of ten years, two while I was a student in training. With no way to measure directly the harm to those more closely involved, I can attest to the lesser, but distinct order of harm to beginning analysts—a sense of wariness and discouragement, if not alienation on the part of students who may feel betrayed by their teachers' actions. These were painful losses for everyone, with reverberations impossible to chart. I will try to navigate between an enervated weariness with the subject, on the one hand, and a strident, self-righteous accusatory tone, on the other.

Let me start a bit obliquely, appraising this material from some distance. I am touched—as the expression goes—by a particular sentence in Elisabeth Young-Bruehl's (1988) biography of Anna Freud, evoking in an image Anna's grief following the death of her friend and companion Dorothy Burlingham: "She also comforted herself by wearing Dorothy's sweaters around the house and stroking these representations of the friend whom no one in their acquaintance had ever seen her caress or embrace" (443). The sentence depicts an eighty-three-year-old grief-stricken woman, who was never seen to touch—affectionately to touch—her companion of over fifty years. Now we see her wearing, and stroking, the dead woman's sweaters, with these reminders of her beloved friend also enfolding, and in the gesture caressing, her.

What exactly is Anna Freud touching? Is she, in stroking the sweater, touching herself, inside that garment? Is she in effect touching her friend who once wore the garment? Is her friend Dorothy somehow inhabiting the sweater, touching her? Certainly the reader is moved by this physical representation of empathy—an example of a writer's art, compactly presentational.

In *Anna Freud: A Biography*, Young-Bruehl avowedly sets out to combine the biographer's "classical mode of writing an edifying exemplary life" (the mode of her Hannah Arendt biography) with a psychoanalyst's focus on the unconscious mind. It is an impossibility, she has said, for the biographer to portray the unconscious mind: the psychoanalyst, unlike the biographer, works with evidences of unconscious mind alive in the room—a patient's dreams, associations, fantasies, transferences (Young-Bruehl 2009: 3).

Thus, the person presented in a psychobiography is "an imagined person, an imaginary person"—as is, we can add, the psychoanalyst.

Young-Bruehl (2009) associates the psychoanalytic biographer's peculiar position with Kierkegaard's figure for irony: it is "like a portrait of an elf wearing the magic cap that makes him invisible" (5). This insight into the writing of a life can usefully be reversed, with biography serving as a way to inspect the peculiar, magnetic, and problematic notion of psychoanalysis itself: in particular, the transference illusion at the center of Sigmund Freud's "talking cure." The image of Anna Freud wearing Dorothy Burlingham's sweater, while stroking it, evokes or epitomizes much about the Freudian enterprise.

Outsides and insides, visible and invisible, cloaking and uncloaking, shielding and revealing. Like biography, psychoanalysis aims to examine a life—to touch without touching, as Anna Freud does with her recently dead friend's garment, in an intricate act of imagination. Psychoanalysis attempts, through words, a gesture of intimacy approaching that of bodily contact. This vocabulary may help illuminate the most queasy, unsettling part of Anna Freud's life story: Sigmund Freud's psychoanalysis of Anna, his twenty-two-year-old daughter. The biographical fact may become more unsettling the more one examines the precise nature of the psychoanalytic engagement.

In the analytic situation two people meet in private and, over time, have an intimate exchange; the medium, again, is words. Their two roles are different, but each entails a promise. The patient pledges to speak with candor—to disclose fantasies, bare secrets, confess wishes—to the analyst who pledges to listen: not to judge but to witness and understand, and to offer back that understanding in a reciprocal gesture. The goal of this verbal process of uncovering one person's latent truths (though both people engage in introspection, and both are moved) is symptom-relief, or healing. The patient's self-disclosure is critical to the success of the treatment, just as is the analyst's understanding, or interpretation.

Freud's much-maligned and misunderstood term "neutrality" captures this special analytic attitude, a benevolent receptivity that has nothing to do with coldness or indifference. The analyst strives for an equal open-minded attentiveness to all that the patient discloses (Freud's "evenly suspended attention"), listening with that sympathetic receptivity fostered by his (or her) neutrality. For the patient, it can be the most open, unguarded intimacy of his or her life—unguarded precisely because the guarding is provided by the "buoys" of Friedman's metaphor, heeded by the navigating clinician.

But why the patient's *pledge* of candor? The patient's pledge to truthful disclosure is fundamental—a given—although at the same time an unachievable ideal. How else, without having made such a pledge, can the patient find the courage to "work through" resistance to the *anxiety* of such disclosing! But there's an additional given—this one an absolute, not an ideal. It is given that the two people carry out this work in abstinence: a central element of the analyst's reciprocal pledge. They do not touch.

The patient speaks with candor and the analyst, impartial and non-interfering, is neither seductive nor seduced. These propositions, articulated by Freud in *Papers on Technique*, amount to technical principles as well as ethical precepts, giving the exchange its efficacy. Freud's inspired essay "Observations on Transference-Love," the sixth and last of the papers, can be read as his methodical argument for abstinence, the fundamental principle upon which treatment rests (as I have noted in Chapter 2). The analyst has "evoked this love by instituting analytic treatment" (Freud 1915a: 169). Abstinence is part of what evokes the love, and adhering to it is an essential requirement. Without the analyst's abstinence—simultaneously a matter of sacred trust and of psychoanalytic technique—there is no treatment. In doing the work, patient and analyst both feel touched, as we say we are by a story or a piece of music; but there is a supervening difference. In André Green's (2005) language, the givens provide an essential structuring third, "a law above the two parties, a law whose observance is necessary for the analysis to take place" (33). It is a state of "intimate separation," in Leo Stone's terms (1961: 90), a "deprivation-in-intimacy" (105), mediated by speech.

Very early in his years-long effort to understand his own discovery, Freud writes the following about "psychical (mental) treatment":

> A layman will no doubt find it hard to understand how pathological disorders of the body and mind can be eliminated by "mere" words. He will feel that he is being asked to believe in magic. And he will not be so very wrong, for the words which we use in our everyday speech are nothing other than watered-down magic.
>
> (1905: 283)

Freud has something to say on other occasions about words, though he presents the verbal exchange as "art" rather than "magic." Below is a passage from his essay "The Exceptions" (the first section of "Some

Character-Types Met with in Psycho-Analytic Work") where he takes the example of Gloucester's opening soliloquy in Shakespeare's *Richard III.* Freud (1916b) wonders, how does Shakespeare "compel our sympathy even with a villain like [Richard]," so that we find in him, "an enormous magnification of something we find in ourselves as well"? (314). We are *like* Richard. How does the poet evoke our empathy? Freud's answer:

> It is … a subtle economy of art in the poet that he does not permit his hero to give open and complete expression to all his secret motives. By this means he obliges us to supplement them; he engages our intellectual activity, diverts it from critical reflection and keeps us firmly identified with his hero. A bungler in his place would give conscious expression to all that he wishes to reveal to us, and would then find himself confronted by our cool untrammeled intelligence, which would preclude any deepening of the illusion.
>
> (1916b: 315)

The "subtle economy of art in the poet," the one who is not a "bungler," is another kind of abstinence. The "bungler" says far too much, and sloppily. Shakespeare's gift for economy and selection allows "deepening of the illusion." He "obliges us to supplement," to imagine, to fill in what Richard's words only hint at. There, in the generous and artful gap, we find inner fellow feeling, and we are touched. Tempting, here, to see an analogy between the poet's art and the analyst's skill, based in the technical principle obliging him to hold back, to abstain from prattle as well as touch, allowing the transference illusion to deepen.

I return now to Anna Freud and the queasy core—her analysis begun when she was twenty-two years old. Young-Bruehl's (1988) account of Anna's analysis is painful to read, with its recurring themes of privacy and invasion of privacy, across the family generations. Many years after the analysis ends, Anna Freud will take on the "dual role of step-parent and psychoanalyst" (138) to Dorothy Burlingham's children.

It is a peculiar legacy: the psychoanalytic history of questionable judgment about clinical boundaries, a misestimation of potential for harm sitting right alongside the genuine and profound power to help. Freud did not have sex with his patient Anna. However, some of his followers did become sexually involved with their patients. What are the effects, across generations and down to our own, of the history of egregious "boundary violations" (the profession's argot for these misdeeds) among the early psychoanalytic practitioners? Anna Freud's analysis was considered a "success" by Freud and indeed by his daughter herself—allowing her to "transform fantasy activity and daydreaming into the social activity of writing" (Young-Bruehl 1988: 107). The analysis, begun in 1918, is interrupted, and resumed in 1924, when the father, now ill with his cancer and unable to travel, suggests to Anna that they take up the analytic work again. She's not yet thirty years old. We might wonder, whose needs are met here, in the father's analysis of this adoring daughter—ascetic, angelic, a "vestal," and the "chief keeper of her father's person" and, for the rest of her life, keeper also of his art or science, psychoanalysis (Young-Bruehl 1988: 137). In 1936, in *The Ego and the Mechanisms of Defense*, Anna Freud gives to over-goodness the name "altruistic surrender."

To whom did Anna Freud, an earnest, intelligent young woman of twenty-two, pledge to tell her secrets? To whom did the barely post-adolescent girl promise to expose herself? For Anna Freud, in the transference, the representative of the parental love object and the actual love object are one and the same. Surely this is too much exposure, too *much* touching, however figurative it may be! Is Freud, as founding-father analyst—what he calls, pejoratively and ironically—an "Exception," like Richard III? It's unsettling to consider how blindered this great thinker is in relation to his own discovery and his own child. Blindered, brilliant, and human, he appointed himself to be an exception, accepting her analytic pledge of transparency. Poets and biographers do this in the name of art—inspecting, and exposing, other people—but most of the time there has been no pledge, no promise to witness without judging, receptive but impartial.

The analyst knows that these two principles—the patient's pledge of candor and his own promise of abstinence—structure a psychoanalytic treatment, setting a process in motion. The structuring givens protect both people, as well as providing a cushion for the inevitable discomfort of the analyst's position. The analyst, as transference magnet, in effect courts the patient's passion: "The process of cure is accomplished," Freud (1907) writes, "in a relapse into love," an indispensable relapse, "for the symptoms on account of which the treatment has been undertaken ... can only be resolved and washed away by a fresh high tide of the same passions" (90).

Since the analyst himself evokes the patient's transference-love, "It is therefore plain to him that he must not derive any personal advantage from it. The patient's willingness makes no difference; it merely throws the whole responsibility on the analyst himself" (Freud 1915a: 164). The analyst's abstinence is *magnetic*, sometimes even dazzling.

In the psychoanalytic process of transference the analyst, then, is not merely innocent (though he holds a sacred trust) but instead deliberate. According to Freud (1915a), "psychoanalytic treatment is founded on truthfulness" (164). How do we reconcile "truthfulness" with an arrangement that activates a psychological seduction? Can a seduction be truthful? Can a father analyze a daughter? Can a daughter be candid, "working through" the anxiety of baring secrets, confessing wishes, to the transference magnet, simultaneously both imaginary person and actual father?

Was harm done? Did Anna's analysis free her, or bind her tighter to him? If both, then in what ways and proportions? Did the analysis enable Anna Freud, a young person with a tendency to obsessional defenses, more flexibly to use these defenses; or did she as a result of the analysis become ruled by them? Or wear them as a functional garment? She became a "virtuoso sublimator" (Young-Bruehl's phrase) of her sexual desires: restricted, ascetic, but at the same time attuned to the sexual life of children—Anna was no puritan. As early as 1930 Anna Freud accords greater importance to childhood incest than did her father. "If her attunement to incest was greater than her father's," asks Bennett Simon (1992), "was it primarily because she had been analyzed by her father or because she had worked with children?" (977).

Freud's analyzing his daughter suggests his underestimation of the complexity of the psychoanalytic exchange, the vehicle for easing human suffering whose power he is only gradually discovering. When father and daughter resume the analysis, he is struggling with the mouth cancer that will eventually kill him—a rotting from inside his organ of communication. Facing his mortality, is Freud the more vulnerable to misjudgment, and self-deception? Anna Freud will devote herself to her father's "immortality," the psychoanalytic movement.

Does Freud use his daughter to further his cause, disavowing the symbolically incestuous? Did he delude himself into taking a god-like role in her life, convinced that he could be "objective" as her analyst—uninvolved, no father, his daughter untouched? The god Zeus too, like Freud, is both father and exception. But unlike Freud, the Olympian is immune to ordinary mortal limit, and endures no reprisal for liberties taken or injury inflicted. The analysis of Anna calls up one's ambivalence about Freud, the exceptional, seminal genius who at the least risked being the kind of self-approving "exception" his essay describes.

With refreshing directness Fidias Cesio, quoting from "Observations on Transference-Love," vigorously rejects Freud's reasoning about the separate "aims" of analyst and patient:

> Freud emphasizes that, if the analyst satisfied the patient's love demands, "the patient would achieve her aim, but he would never achieve his" (1915, p. 165). We find this statement questionable and feel that it is the other way round. Experience shows that it is usually the analyst who in these cases achieves his neurotic aim, for, if he remains within the setting, this outcome is precluded. The patient's "aim" is to find relief for her neurotic suffering.
>
> (Cesio 1993: 141)

Cesio's cogent remarks, reversing Freud's formulation, apply to the long history of clinicians recklessly mixing psychoanalysis with sexual involvement as if that mix held no contradiction.

Notorious instances among Freud's contemporaries include Sandor Ferenczi's falling in love with his analysand Elma Palos—she is also his mistress's daughter!—and sending her off to Freud for treatment in the hope of becoming her husband (Hughes 2004: 18), as well as Carl Jung's involvement with Sabina Spielrein. Freud (1915a) himself is unequivocal on the contradiction as a technical matter: "The love-relationship in fact destroys the patient's susceptibility to influence from analytic treatment. A combination of the two would be an impossibility" (166). But beyond the technical consequence of "impossibility," there are moral consequences.

...

Sexual misconduct as a catastrophic breach of the therapeutic contract has been more widely recognized in recent decades. An issue of *Psychoanalytic Inquiry* published in 1997 contains several essays representative of how, after nearly a century of avoidance and denial, the profession of psychoanalysis has begun to think about the problem of the analyst's misconduct. The writing in this issue characterizes the approach to the subject in a literature that has grown dramatically in the last twenty years. The seven essays in the volume were presentations at a 1994 symposium titled "New Psychoanalytic Perspectives on the

Treatment of Sexual Trauma." Two of the papers specifically address the subject of therapist-patient sexual involvement. A third contribution, by Glen Gabbard, discusses these two.

In the volume's prologue, the editor, Howard Levine (1997b), notes that the papers "are among the first published psychoanalytic attempts to examine the experience, motivations, and treatment of cases of patient-therapist sexual boundary violations" (240)—an astonishing fact, he acknowledges, given the reality, throughout the history of psychoanalysis, not only of temptations but of many actual transgressions: the analyst's sexual exploitation of the transference. Freud's aim in 1915, in "Observations on Transference-Love," as we have seen, is to address that same danger, ever present because built into the situation.

Gabbard (1997), one of the most forthright authors to tackle the subject of the analyst's sexual transgression, also remarks on how long it has taken to acknowledge the reality: "For too long the 'old boy' network of psychoanalysis appeared to have much greater interest in protecting their own members than in addressing the needs of the patients" in this "professional form of incest" (379). In another of the articles, Marvin Margolis (1997) echoes Gabbard: "Our institutional timidity has made us complicit and a party to the abuse of these patients" (351). Although fear of litigation is one factor behind secrecy and silence, a deeper one, Margolis believes, lies in "our horror of actual violations of the incest taboo which is at the psychological core of these boundary violations" (350).

It is natural to want to look away, and there is also a risk for those who insist on bringing the problem into the open: "Some colleagues who take up this cause," writes Margolis (1997), "assume considerable professional risk within their own group as their motives and judgment are questioned, even at times impugned" (350). He concludes: "Our past neglect of the area of sexual boundary violations has contributed to an image of professionals who circle the wagons to protect colleagues who have transgressed sexually with their patients while ignoring the distress of their victims" (369).

Such strong declarations are deeply admirable but at the same time perhaps so commonplace, even pro forma, as to evoke a yawn. Perhaps the reader's yawn (I include my own) is also self-protective and, like the profession's silence, complicit: it deflects attention from the ugliness—in Margolis' terms, the "horror." The shock of recognizing that for decades the caregivers put their own protection first in a caregiving profession is diminished by its familiarity. We may read past the words because of how frequently such failures are reported, not only in the professions but in the larger culture, which until recently has blindered itself to marital rape and the sexual exploitation of children. Outrage and helplessness are dampened by a sense of repetition.

Janet Wohlberg, in her essay in the same issue of *Psychoanalytic Inquiry*, writes from another perspective: as someone who has been sexually exploited by a therapist. The founder of a self-help group for women who have been sexually involved with their therapists, Wohlberg has heard many individual accounts. Considering the similarities (and differences) between a patient's violation by a therapist and a child's violation by an adult, she notes that such acts "occur in significantly power-imbalanced relationships." Wohlberg (1997) echoes Freud in restating the obvious but essential point: "patient-therapist sex is always the responsibility of the therapist" (329).

Wohlberg's vivid examples dispel yawns. Although sexual relations with her therapist did not begin for three years, she understands in retrospect that the route to disaster had been paved early. (This "route to disaster" is referred to in the literature with an inadvertently suggestive and dismissive cliché, the "slippery slope".) She remembers that Dr. S often chose to focus on her sexual needs and fantasies despite her wish to talk about other things. He also took phone calls during her hours and breached the confidentiality of other patients. The narrative includes the comically grotesque—in the range of transgressive behaviors, a repellent extreme, far more drastic than what Gabbard has described as the "lovesick" analyst who exploits a patient: "Adding to the picture was Dr. S's collection of exotic pets. On several occasions, his owl regurgitated chicken bones onto the office floor, and at one point, a snake escaped from its terrarium and slithered across my feet" (Wohlberg 1997: 325). Wohlberg cites another extreme example (from the report of a case in Massachusetts: *Board of Registration in Medicine v. Edward M. Daniels, M.D.*, 1991):

> Dr. Daniels used condoms. And he insisted that I buy those condoms … that was one of the most humiliating parts of the whole thing for me … because I was very embarrassed and very terrified to walk into drugstores to have to buy condoms … He would put them in Kleenex and … wad them up and then he gave them to me to go in to his

bathroom to flush them down the toilet. And he stood there to watch to make sure I did it, but he never walked out with them himself.

(Wohlberg 1997: 337)

Freud (1916b) tries to feel his way into the grandiosity behind such human cruelty as this when he writes, in the aggrieved Gloucester's voice, "I have a right to be an exception, to disregard the scruples by which others let themselves be held back. I may do wrong myself since wrong has been done to me." If only we could see deeply enough into Gloucester's deprivation and suffering, and find in the villain "an enormous magnification of something we find in ourselves" (314), we could perhaps make some sense of his perceived "right." Perhaps we could make sense of the analyst's self-delusional "right" to exploit, humiliate, and wound.

It's important to make clear that I am not equating behaviors, nor do I intend to neatly distinguish among them. Gabbard's "lovesick" analyst is certainly not the same as Dr. S, or Dr. Daniels, but we also cannot know, with certitude, exactly how he is different; nor can we determine tidily what separates the analyst who abstains from the one who gives way. I'm less concerned here to consider nuanced degrees in a range of pathologies and behaviors, or to construct categories of unethical conduct, than I am to inspect the risks and vulnerabilities *inherent* to the psychoanalytic situation—the greatest of these, perhaps, the tendency to find certainty when the only certain thing is our human capacity for self-deception, and sometimes self-delusion.

It is arguable, perhaps, that such exploitation of patients, if not eradicated (or ever eradicable), is now better controlled, given the attention focused on it. The profession expresses not only awareness of ethical breaches since the time of Freud but also better understands the harmfulness, and acknowledges its neglect, for decades, of responsibility for the patient's safety. With acknowledgment (an argument might go), there is greater protection. Essays are written about the subject, journals are devoted to it, symposia address it, and unpleasant examples—like the extreme ones above—are made public.

And psychoanalysis (it might be argued further), with its understanding of the ubiquitous tendency to repeat—an idea fundamental to the psychoanalytic view—is well equipped to guard against repetition. But that expectation may underestimate the "open sea" of Friedman's metaphor that begins this essay. In *Boundaries and Boundary Violations in*

Psychoanalysis, one of the first books attempting to address the subject, Gabbard and Lester speak to the power, across analytic generations, of this unwanted repetition:

> the intergenerational transmission of attitudes about the concept of boundaries can be extraordinarily powerful. In the mid-1960s, a training analyst ... was charged with sexual misconduct. Two decades later, two analysts he had analyzed were also charged with sexual misconduct in the same city. Blind spots in one analytic generation may well become blind spots in the next.
>
> (1995: 86)

Such is the power of repetition, even of moral blindness or self-delusion, from one generation to the next, that it conceivably may be transmitted like a birth defect. It's reasonable to expect that recognition of that power produces alertness. But the question must be asked, at what point does acknowledgment shade into complacency? Can a profession's acknowledgment of past lapses become itself a form of grandiosity or self-congratulation? Without the analyst's moral integrity, there is no treatment. Building on Freud's propositions in *Papers on Technique*, Macalpine writes in 1950 that the analyst's moral integrity "becomes a safeguard for the patient to proceed with analysis; it is a technical device and not a moral precept" (527). With these unsentimental words, she calls not for apologies or expressions of good intentions, but for stringent intellectual scrutiny. The presence or absence of Macalpine's "technical device" is an ethical matter: in the psychoanalytic situation, moral integrity is the ultimate safeguard.

In the editor's epilogue to that 1997 issue of *Psychoanalytic Inquiry*, Levine slips into some troubling language in small but crucial matters of emphasis and clarity:

> One only need think of Breuer and Anna O., Jung and Sabina Spielrein, Ferenczi and Elma Palos, and too many other analytic couples to realize that falling in love with one's patient or analyst is not only an occupational hazard, but one which carries with it the real danger of being acted upon ... While we deplore the destructive consequences of such actions, we take pride in being able to publish two of the first contributions to the psychoanalytic literature on this subject.
>
> (1997a: 390)

Mainly, this is an admirable statement. However, Levine's formulations reveal a degree of conceptual blur, or deflection, in contrast with Ida Macalpine's crispness.

That is, while falling in love with one's patient is indeed an "occupational hazard" for the therapist—a hazard historically proven—it is not true that the hazard of falling in love with one's analyst is "occupational" for the patient; the patient seeks a professional service and rightfully expects protection in a life-changing drama that intentionally courts risk. This is more than a quibble: the psychoanalytic situation is carefully structured to foster the hazard of attachment—the essential vehicle through which the patient gets what is paid for. Cesio's point is similar in questioning Freud's thinking about the "aims" of analyst and patient: the patient has come for analysis, and the patient's vulnerability is central to the psychoanalytic conception and to healing. "The cure," Freud (1906) himself writes, "is effected by love" (quoted in McGuire 1974: 12–13).

Coming after this passage, in which the roles and obligation of clinician and patient are blurred, the sentence's grammatical subordination ("While we deplore the destructive consequences … we take pride in being able to publish …") becomes part of an unfortunate context, emphasizing communal self-congratulation. Little solecisms such as the misapplied term "occupational hazard" and a regrettable grammatical structure perhaps embody, precisely, the fraught and paradoxical nature of the psychoanalytic enterprise, with its sensitivity to opposites and human contradictions.

The analyst's merely mortal limitation is an ever-present threat to capsize the psychoanalytic situation; and at the same time the analyst's ordinary humanness—the particularity of his or her person, with all its flaws—is the necessary vehicle of treatment. Underlying *Papers on Technique*, as I have noted, is the implicit paradox of *abstinence as alluring*: the principle of abstinence protects but, by design, also heats the crucible—thus conflating the ethical and the technical. Macalpine's point is similar.

The profession has neglected certain problematic truths about the psychoanalytic engagement. Two people repeatedly alone, in private, more or less inevitably develop feelings for each other; and the analyst—in the role of transference magnet on a stage purposely tilted to court the patient's passion—has the position of power and responsibility. Given this fact, the analyst's moral integrity is the patient's ultimate safeguard. But here we must pause. As Thomas Szasz (1963) states, "No one, psychoanalysts included, has as yet discovered a method to make people behave with integrity when no one is watching. Yet this is the kind of integrity that analytic work requires of the analyst" (435). There is no conceivable test one takes during training, or at any time, to neatly measure integrity. Nor is integrity a fixed and incorruptible element in any human being.

•••

Victor Calef and Edward Weinshel (1980) write that the analyst serves as "the conscience of the analysis," a function they describe as "super-ordinate" to all other component activities: the analyst is the "keeper of the analytic process" (279). A "keeper" is one who protects, or has the charge or care of something. Calef and Weinshel propose that through the training analysis a candidate develops the capacity to serve as conscience. Without that capacity, the future analyst is in danger, they assert, of "using analysis as a tool to be directed against others instead of for them and for oneself" (289).

I believe Donald Winnicott is in the same territory when he says that there are certain risks—for Winnicott (1969), these risks are the analyst's death and the analyst's retaliation—"that simply must be taken by the patient" (714). The risks of someone dying or retaliating come with the analyst's being human, and the analyst's task, in Winnicott's language, is "to survive" being used by the patient, with his (or her) psychoanalytic technique intact (714).

Winnicott (1969) is careful, however, not to equate these risks: "even the actual death of the analyst is not as bad," he writes, "as the development in the analyst of a change of attitude towards retaliation" (714). Implicit is the idea, again paradoxical, that the analyst who dies during treatment may "survive"—in the more essential sense of intact analytic function—while the analyst who retaliates—the one whose psychoanalytic technique is compromised—fails and, in another sense, "dies." To stay with Winnicott's terms, the analyst's sexual exploitation of the patient is perhaps the most extreme retaliation, though human payback may of course take infinite forms. Might the analyst's silence or unresponsiveness, for example, sometimes manifest a form of revenge—a hurtful, at times cruel rigidity masquerading as technical correctness?

I have called the analyst's silence "an upside-down breach of the analytic frame—he is not too loose but instead too tight and unbending"

(Pinsky 2014a: 15). In that particular instance, a patient, Leigh, has ended a productive five-year analysis. Three months after this end, she phones the analyst, Dr. O, and leaves a message:

> with news about her child who had been sick, with cancer, and whose illness, treatment and impending recovery coincide with the end of the analysis. Leigh calls to leave happy news, wanting the analyst to know that the child, in a followup medical exam, has been declared well. Dr. O doesn't return the call, nor does he respond to the patient's note expressing bewilderment and distress: it was as if the analyst had fallen off the face of the earth. Eventually, Dr. O explains his silence: he did not want to be intrusive.
>
> (Pinsky 2014a: 14–15)

Has the analyst retaliated? On an imagined continuum of harmful behaviors, such a failure to respond is relatively mild. But on the continuum of enactments, or of Winnicott's countertransference hatred, this analyst's punitive (if not vindictive) silence surely finds a place. The patient, as Winnicott says, must take the risk: the analyst—a human vehicle—may die, or may retaliate.

In Guy Thompson's (2004) view, "When Freud conceived countertransference, he [had] one principal concern: that of insuring the protection of the patient from abuse by the analyst" (107). One recognizes that concern in "Observations on Transference-Love" (1915)—the true topic of Freud's early essay, as I argue elsewhere, is the countertransference, though mentioned almost in passing.[2] Thompson cogently likens Winnicott's notion of professional attitude to Freud's principle of neutrality. "Hence countertransference, properly speaking," Thompson writes, "alludes to a failure on the part of the analyst: that of insuring a necessary boundary between patient and analyst. Whereas Freud characterizes this attitude as one of neutrality, Winnicott characterizes it as one of professionalism" (107).

If a crucial capacity—call it maintaining one's integrity, "surviving" as analyst, serving as "conscience of the analysis," or striving for "neutrality"—is developed and handed down through the generations, analyst to student, then the same capacity logically should reside first in the training analyst, a fact that may in the end offer the patient only another set of boxes within boxes, or Russian nesting dolls. A watchman to watch the watchman is fine, but principles or conceptual structures are necessary too, as Freud well understood in *Papers on Technique*. It is noteworthy that egregious violators are often the most visible and respected "trainers" themselves—including, not many years ago, the chair of the American Psychoanalytic Association's national Ethics Committee. Whatever this says about "training" and "trainers," it does suggest the Olympian delusion, and Freud's notion of "exceptions."

What can failures of ethical conduct tell us about the nature of the psychoanalytic exchange, the risks for the patient, and the particular stresses and temptations confronting the psychoanalyst? Emphasizing the closeness of the psychoanalytic encounter to the Oedipal situation, Otto Kernberg describes the inevitable tension of "an intimacy in which there is a prohibition on sexual expression on top of which there is also a discussion of the sexual aspect of this intimacy." He comments further (in another regrettable note of communal self-congratulation): "It is the most intense potential seduction, and we can congratulate ourselves that we have no more than one percent of boundary transgressions" (quoted in Bergmann 2004: 297). Kernberg's statistic understates the reality, particularly in dyads where the analyst is a man and the patient a younger woman.[3]

The psychoanalytic situation is a professional encounter structured to invite intense transference reactions—at times in both people—with the purpose of understanding them for the benefit of the patient. What makes analytic transference feelings different from non-analytic ones is that the analyst, in a difficult balancing act, strives neither to act on these feelings nor to be indifferent to them, a stance that allows them to flourish, be experienced, and examined. In "Remembering, Repeating and Working-Through"—the fifth of the *Papers on Technique*—Freud focuses on the patient's experience intensely lived out in the treatment. Always implicit in Freud's formulations, in my view, is the analyst's experience: the counterpart to the patient's.

In this well-known essay Freud introduces the notion of "working-through" (along with the concept of "compulsion to repeat," obviously relevant to my considerations here), linking it with the resistance: "One must allow the patient time to become more conversant with this resistance with which he has now become acquainted," Freud (1914b) writes, "to work through it, to overcome it, by continuing, in defiance of it, the analytic work according to the fundamental rule of analysis" (155). The arduous process of working-through now defines the course of treatment: it is through coming to know the resistance and, in spite of its imperative force, to defy it, that the patient changes. *Papers on Technique* grew out of Freud's increasing appreciation and understanding (are the papers Freud's own "working-through"?) of two people's engagement—the analyst "working in common with his patient" (1914b: 155)—and of the pressures and temptations confronting the analyst in the raised temperatures of the exchange.

A distinction may be useful here. Although the principles of neutrality and abstinence, introduced in "Observations on Transference-Love" (the final *Paper*), are interrelated, neutrality is more concerned with how the analyst brings his thoughts to bear on what he witnesses—with how he *attends*—while the rule of abstinence more specifically addresses the analyst's management of *affect*: "abstinence is the effort entailed in resisting a patient's demand for love," writes Thompson (2004), the rule pertaining "exclusively to those feelings that prompt analysts to behave seductively" (52). This is a view of abstinence very different from the caricature of the cartoon analyst's detached and depriving stance. When understood this way, the terms "abstinence" and "neutrality", rather than comprising absence or rigidity, together capture the analyst's extraordinary attitude: a receptive *presence* that includes his physical and social posture in the treatment room.

That unusual situation of course produces tension in both parties. The psychoanalytic situation, by its structure, puts great pressure on certain human traits, constantly tempting the analyst's grandiosity: the patient is dazzled by transference invitation, and the analyst invited to feel that he is dazzling. The analyst who explains his consulting room activity by saying, "'I only analyze,'" Henry Smith (2006) writes, "may be courageously trying to keep his or her eye on the ball despite the genuine affects flooding the field. As everyone knows, restraint of impulse is a slender reed" (688). The passage's mixed metaphors—the ball, the flood, the reed—can perhaps be read as one more indicator of anxiety provoked by the affect-laden situation.

What will guide the analyst in such treacherous waters? *Papers on Technique* offers Freud's early attempt to work out an answer. If behind the consulting room door the struggling analyst behaves, knowingly or unknowingly, as if he or she is all-powerful—an "exception," like Freud's Richard III, or immortal, like Zeus himself—and exempt from the restrictions and guiding principles that bind other people, then both patient and therapist are in jeopardy. Here is a quotation from a psychoanalytic paper about the analyst's death to further exemplify the human readiness for self-delusion and for idealization: "Mr. L. remarked that you can't expect even psychoanalysts to be superhuman, especially when they are dying" (Freedman 1990: 308). The sentence reveals a tendency—located in the word "even"—for the profession, as well as the patient (Mr. L.), to elevate the therapist as someone above certain vulnerabilities of body and mind, god-like. The roots of this delusion are both theoretical and experiential, fostered not only in the theory underlying the situation, but in the experience of analyst and patient too.

Theories of the psychoanalytic situation and of the analyst's role tend to emphasize the uniqueness of both: it is no ordinary exchange. The analytic relationship, as I have said, is like no other, a notion articulated first by Freud in 1915 in specific reference to the analyst's handling of the patient's transference love. The doctor's course, Freud (1915a) writes there, "is one for which there is no model in real life" (166). In Friedman's metaphor, the buoys mark out that "course." To give shape to the analyst, one compares that person—both ordinary and without peer (or model)—to something known. That simile coining is exactly what Freud and his followers did, and continue to do, as analyst and analytic interaction are conceived and reconceived, now for over a hundred years: for example, in historical, chronological order, from the analyst as reflecting mirror (Freud), to a guardian-like figure safe-keeping a vision (Loewald), to a participant in a mutual self-inquiry (Gardner), to a skilled assistant (Poland), to a surfer riding a wave (Renik). With that sequence, the endeavor becomes more collaborative, the analyst—so it seems—more affectively involved, and the patient and therapist more explicitly, and mutually, swept up by the situation. (These and other similes and metaphors for the analyst and the psychoanalytic process are the subject of Chapter 5.)

Although a therapeutic relationship may not be exactly like any other, it of course also resembles other relationships. The analyst is not *exactly* like the teacher or the parent or the dermatologist, but there are similarities, even in the instance of the skin doctor. However, we don't find education experts insistently reminding us that the student-teacher bond is unique, nor is there quite comparable debate about the role of the teacher. Yet that pedagogical bond is also unique, and the teacher, like the therapist, in a position of sacred trust. In the discomfort revealed by the reminding, and the redefining, we can again detect the dilemma of elevating the analyst's role, so difficult to conceptualize, to a special realm, *apart*. While shifts in theory, and in the figurative language that reflects theory, represent efforts to grapple with the difficulty (as we see, for example, in the growth of countertransference theory, enactment theory, and the contemporary analyst's removal increasingly from a position of authority), the problem is not so easily solved.

A second root of the delusion elevating the therapist is experiential, and entwined with the first. As well as being human, the analyst in the specialized situation may take on what Fliess (1942) calls a "rare and exalted perfection" (225). For the patient, the tendency to elevate the therapist to the realm of invulnerability is understandable, even invited, given the structure of the situation, the task for each person, and the place of illusion if their shared work is to get done. That same tendency, if it lulls the therapist (encouraging him to feel that he is dazzling), is less benign. Arnold Modell writes about the essential place of illusion:

> For both therapist and patient, the other person is experienced both as an individual in ordinary life and as someone transformed by the therapeutic process, a [transformation] we label as transference and countertransference. Therapist and patient are also everyday people, but within the frame of the therapeutic process an illusion is created that can be described as another level of reality.
>
> (1991: 15)

The dangers of benign illusion, however, must be looked at. What kinds of beings are these who, within the therapeutic setting, inhabit "another level of reality"? They are at every moment in that habitation no less real, no less ordinary "everyday" people. If the therapist, who is supposed to guard the process, loses sight of the idealization—we call it an "as-if," a benign and temporary illusion—then the therapist has embraced an Olympian stance. That delusion, even if it has no other harmful effects, impedes the patient's necessary *dis*illusion: a gradual process of mourning that includes acceptance of the analyst as a human being with ordinary defects and limitations. Indeed, only an imperfect, striving mortal can *offer* the doubled gifts of attention and abstinence. A god, or a machine, can't do it.

Another seed of the thinking that elevates the therapist to superhuman can be traced to Freud's early optimism about the psychoanalytic method and its potential for producing perfect health: Weinshel's "the myth of perfectibility." More recently, Kantrowitz (2015) locates a similar tendency to construct myths of perfection in the termination literature. "These myths," she writes, "create expectations about how analyses should end that may be passed from generation to generation … the idea of a 'perfect' analytic ending remains, and many analysts reveal this as a core belief," evident in their analytic conference presentations or, "more troubling," in the classroom (1). In the counterpart of such myths, we may posit an analyst who is superman or superwoman: a magician, someone who has the capacity as healer to create mortal perfection. The myth of the fully analyzed analyst (or of a perfect analysis), far from disappearing—the same myth implied in Mr. L.'s "even a psychoanalyst"—lives on in conceptions of the analyst with superhuman capacity to do the demanding work.[4]

Having abandoned his hopes for the attainment of perfect health, Freud wrote in 1937, straightforward and modest in the claim, "Analysts are people who have learned to practice a particular art; alongside of this, they may be allowed to be human beings like anyone else" (247). But what happens if the analyst himself denies his own human nature—if he denies or suppresses the realities of anxiety, anger, desire, temptation, fatigue, sadness, ill health? Self-effacement, too, can become a form of self-idealization; an illusory erasing of the self brings the corollary danger of erasing the other—not entirely different from the analyst who becomes wholly preoccupied with his own inner states. While we are all vulnerable, by our human nature, to the delusion of omnipotence, it doesn't follow that we are equally vulnerable to acting on it: "What we do with our impulses," writes Shengold (1991), "makes all the difference" (166).

The more the therapist believes in an heroic capacity for selfless service to the patient, and the more he's conceptualized as above being a subject himself, the greater the danger of erasing the line that keeps the patient safe. Where there's only one entity, there can be no separation. The Olympian delusion is encouraged by a monolithic subjectivity. Since subjectivity is never unilateral in reality, and there are *always* two people present—as Freud recognizes and, in *Papers on Technique*, essays to understand—self-effacement can invert itself and become a tyranny, perhaps even a visitation as bull or swan or eagle. That eventuality is in absolute contrast to the prudent navigator who steers his course, humbly using the buoys to estimate the boundaries of safety.

…

I have tried to distinguish between what I view as Freud's misguided behavior in analyzing his daughter Anna and the abusing analyst's sexual exploitation of a patient. I've suggested a limited but significant overlap between the two: a legacy of misjudgment, even self-delusion, located in Freud's choice. My purpose is not simply to indict Freud, whose decisions are set in the context of human vulnerability, including the struggle to understand his own discovery and his ambition for his project; instead, I've tried to consider some of the risks inherent to the psychoanalytic exchange—risks Freud partially understood in writing *Papers on Technique*—and the effect of his misjudgment on later generations. The same genius who in 1910 explained "transference" as a re-experiencing of "old wishful phantasies" in relation to the physician (51), and who in 1914 articulated the need for the patient's early experience symbolically lived out in the treatment—the concept of "working-through"—a few years later analyzed his daughter. How does a daughter intensely relive "old wishful phantasies" with her father in treatment?

What was Freud thinking, or what was he unable to think—deluded, in the instance of his child? In the same period that he was analyzing Anna, Freud (1926) wrote about patient and analyst: "Nothing takes place between them except that they talk to each other" (187). Did he believe that "words only"—the abstinent attitude that protects but at the same time fosters the unique analytic attachment—meant "untouched"? I began by saying that I would raise more questions than I would answer. In concluding, I return to examining tones and overtones, using a piece of Freud's correspondence with Carl Jung to reprise the concerns and questions I've tried to raise—though aware I haven't answered them.

In 1908 Freud's disciple Jung became intensely involved with a former patient, Sabina Spielrein. When Jung attempted to end the tempestuous affair in the spring of 1909 (it remains unclear whether the relationship was consummated), a furious Spielrein flew at him, knife in hand, and, in the scuffle drew some blood (Carotenuto 1982: 97). In these same years (1906–1913), Freud and Jung were engaged in frequent exchanges of letters. Although Freud had not yet completed *Papers on Technique*, he was surely puzzling over the problems they would address for his science, yet in its baby stage—such fundamental questions as: How is the analyst to find his way in this power-imbalanced situation that invites emotional heat yet has no model? How is he to conduct himself? How to listen, how to attend? What restraints, guides, and resting places when he is affectively touched and, inevitably, confused, pressed, and tempted?

Although not yet aware of Jung's involvement with Spielrein, Freud was already aware in the spring of 1909 that Jung was upset about a former woman patient who, by Jung's account, was spreading scandalous rumors about him. Jung wrote Freud that he had been under great strain, the "last and worst straw" involving "a woman patient, whom years ago I pulled out of a sticky neurosis with greatest devotion," only to have her "kick up a vile scandal solely because I denied myself the pleasure of giving her a child." In other words, she is vindictive; he is beyond reproach, even magnanimous—denying himself a pleasure. Declaring his innocence, Jung adds, "I have always acted the gentleman towards her" (McGuire 1974: 207). In his reply, Freud commiserates with Jung about the forces with which the analyst contends: "To be slandered and scorched by the love with which we operate—such are the perils of our trade, which we are certainly not going to abandon on their account" (McGuire 1974: 210).

In early June of 1909, when Spielrein, still beside herself with rage and grief, wrote to Freud asking to meet with him "about something of greatest importance to me" (Kerr 1993: 217), Freud immediately sent her letter to Jung, asking him who she was and what she wanted. "Weird!" he wrote. "What is she? A busybody, a chatterbox, or a paranoiac?" (Kerr 1993: 218). With historical perspective, we can note the triangle (Freud-Spielrein-Jung), and might recognize Freud's participation in an "enactment"—the current vocabulary for transference and countertransference entanglement. Although Jung knows Spielrein is threatening to expose him, he doesn't acknowledge the truth of his involvement. Instead, he again describes his generosity and the suffering his kindness brought. Jung explains that Spielrein had been his first patient:

> for which reason I remembered her with special gratitude and affection. Since I knew from experience that she would immediately relapse if I withdrew my support, I prolonged the relationship over the years … until I saw an unintended wheel had started turning, whereupon I finally broke with her. She was, of course, systematically planning my seduction, which I considered inopportune. Now she is seeking revenge … To none of my patients have I extended so much friendship and from none have I reaped so much sorrow.
>
> (McGuire 1974: 228–229)

In his response, now well known, Freud extends Jung sympathy and consolation:

> Such experiences, though painful, are necessary and hard to avoid. Without them we cannot know life and what we are dealing with. I myself have never been taken in quite so badly, but I have come very close to it a number of times and had a *narrow escape*. I believe that only grim necessities weighing on my work, and the fact that I was ten years older than yourself when I came to psychoanalysis, have saved me from similar experiences. But no lasting harm is done. They help us to develop the thick skin we need and to dominate "countertransference," which is after all a permanent problem for us; they teach us to displace our own affects to best advantage. They are a *blessing in disguise*.
>
> (McGuire 1974: 230–231, emphasis in original)

As Freud was becoming more clear during these years about the inevitability of the analyst's own affective experience in the treatment, his letter is of interest partly because the word "countertransference" appears here for the first time. Of even greater interest, however, is the remarkable absence in the passage of Sabina Spielrein as a human being.

Neither named nor embodied—there is no pronoun in the passage that refers to her—Spielrein is present as part of an experience: "Such experiences, though painful, are necessary and hard to avoid." Vague and impersonal, almost abstract, she is like a force of nature, and impossible to resist, at least for a young man. This Spielrein might as well be a mythological figure, a siren or Medusa, serving as a vehicle (an object) for the analyst's painful but necessary lesson. The experience helps him "develop the thick skin" to protect him from the temptations and provocations of the clinical exchange. A few years later, in 1915, Freud will write "Observations on Transference-Love"—addressed to the young and inexperienced doctor. Properly understood, perhaps the rule of abstinence is Freud's later, more considered, language for developing the "thick skin" he refers to in the letter to Jung.

In assuring Jung that "no lasting harm is done" and that the experience can be turned to advantage—"a blessing in disguise"—Freud moves the doctor's well-being, along with the betterment of psychoanalysis itself, to the center of attention. The patient is consigned to being a means to a greater good. Lofty, detached—and apparently ignoring the woman's reality—these Jung-Freud letters suggest an Olympian conversation.

To Freud's credit, he didn't know the entire truth at this point, although eventually Jung confessed to him, "a guilty admission of everything except intercourse" (Kerr 1993: 221). Freud's vanity in the passage is attached to his vision of psychoanalysis, and his ambition, which may blind him to the possibility that Jung is capable of deception—Freud's own idealization. He assumes Jung is innocent rather than complicit, and subject to Spielrein's systematic seduction and vengefulness. Jung is the focus of attention (his own and Freud's), while the patient Spielrein vanishes. To repeat a fundamental paradox: the pretense or delusion that there is only one subjectivity in the room results in an annihilation. Only the Olympian presence remains.

...

The same discipline Freud protects in the correspondence with Carl Jung came, eventually, into the care of his daughter Anna. *Anna Freud: A Biography* returns, for its closing scene, to the image of a garment: cloaking yet expressive, protective yet intrusive, touching while enshrouding. The scene includes Manna Friedmann, the German-speaking retired nursery school teacher—the *Kinderfrau*—who helps take care of the dying Anna. Anna's friend Dorothy has been dead three years. Manna Friedman takes her Anna for outings from the hospital in a wheelchair—"happy outings," Young-Bruehl writes, in these last days full of misery. Then:

> While they were planning one of their excursions for the next day, the summer weather was turning cooler. Struggling for words, Anna Freud asked Manna Friedmann to stop by 20 Maresfield Gardens on her way to the hospital: she would find hanging in Anna Freud's bedroom closet the Professor's Lodenmantel, which had been ritualistically cleaned and refurbished every year since the end of the war. Then, when they went off to the park, the Kinderfrau and Anna Freud, she, shrunken to the size of a schoolgirl, sat wrapped inside her father's big wool coat.
>
> (1988: 453)

Notes

1 This text originally appeared, in a slightly different version, in *Journal of the American Psychoanalytic Association* 59(2) (2011): 351–375. Some portions also appeared earlier in a piece titled "Dress," in *Salmagundi*, Summer 2010. Reprinted with permission.
2 I elaborate this point in Chapters 2 and 4.
3 Celenza writes: "the prevalence studies consistently show an overrepresentation of male therapists who report having engaged in sexual boundary violations. In general, studies report 7–9% male therapists while female therapists account for only 2–3% of the incidence rate" (2007: 6).
4 McLaughlin wryly states: "The Panel on selection of candidates for analytic training collectively provided such an array of aptitudes to be sought in the budding analyst that to one participant suggested a composite portrait of Pasteur and Thomas Mann" (1981: 651). That is a portrait of the candidate *before* the training analysis.

Chapter 4

The Instrument[1]

[A] limit of time is fixed for thee, which if thou dost not use for clearing away the clouds from the mind, it will go and thou wilt go, and it will never return.

—Marcus Aurelius, *Meditations, Book 2*

The haunting image of a diminished Anna Freud wrapped in her father's *Lodenmantel* embodies the most poignant human form of transience: mortality. The guardian of his project, as well as a captive, Anna herself is dying, and the familiar person is no longer there for comfort. As with Dorothy Burlingham's sweater, the father's absence has heightened the meaning of the garment enfolding her: an example of Freud's "scarcity value in time."

His brief essay with that phrase at its core, "On Transience" (1916), contains fewer than thirteen hundred words. It contains no clinical material. Nevertheless, in significant ways, it can be argued that few papers in Freud's entire body of work are *more* relevant to the clinical situation than this account of a summer walk with friends in the mountains. As Matthew Von Unwerth (2005) suggests in his rich examination of Freud's essay, the walk likely never happened: "The afternoon walk, it turns out, may not have been a walk at all," writes Von Unwerth, "nor can one find in the Dolomites the place where the companions met" (3–4). The scene is Freud's invention, a fiction he presents as recollection in order to capture the centrality of loss and the universal experience of grief, with its requisite painful mourning.

Freud writes "On Transience" as part of a commemorative volume honoring the poet Goethe. A meditation on sorrow, beautifully written and conversational, even tender, in tone, "On Transience" is itself an act of mourning. Mourning, like writing itself, is in Freud's terms a form of working-through (1914b), that central concept of the clinical process only briefly and ambiguously defined by Freud, but at the same time identifying the necessary task for patient as well as analyst, though their roles differ. The asymmetrical situation is structured to foster the patient's intensity of attachment to the analyst, and a reciprocal bond, in some form, must hold. How do two people, involved in this peculiar and intimate way, separate and say goodbye? Indeed, if an analysis takes on the depth that makes it successful, one might wonder how either partner can tolerate ending, with the mourning entailed.

Mourning, writing, working-through—here is an extremely compact example of all three, and their overlap: a short poem by Ben Jonson, the great seventeenth-century playwright and poet. Titled "To the Reader," Jonson's poem, a single sentence, comprises two lines—a couplet—twenty-one words in all, counting the title:

To the Reader
Pray thee, take care, that tak'st my book in hand
To read it well—that is, to understand.

The words are all monosyllabic, until the final, three-syllable "understand." One can readily hear the effect of that careful arrangement, a little, emphatic explosion of syllables to end the sentence. Here is the power of form— the brevity, and the deliberate arrangement of word sounds for emphasis, are among the poem's formal elements. It's swift, and economical, and it moves: There's a foray out (line 1) and a quick return (line 2). There's also rhyme: three vivid words, "book in hand," rhyme with the single word "understand." Contained in the rhyme is the poet's essential meaning, his instruction, or plea, to the reader: "book in hand ... understand." Elements like these—rhyme, word order, speed—build emotional force toward that all-important final word: to *understand*. What is the poet mourning? Perhaps that any sufficiency of the relationship between poet and poem, or between writer and book, is in a sense lost forever once the work of art is presented to the world. With the couplet the poet releases the book: it's no longer his entirely, nor in the same way. The poem too is no longer his; in completing it, he lets it go and, like the book, it belongs now to the reader.

Technique—poetic, rhetorical, clinical—*gets at* experience, conscious and unconscious. The reader addressed in Jonson's title can be likened to the analyst, and the book he (or she) takes in hand likened to the articulated experience of the patient who's come for understanding: the patient says, "I ask you, my analyst, to take care to read well what I say, and *how*." That is, to understand. As to form, though Freud himself was an expert writer, and certainly interested in poetic effects (1908), he'd likely agree that the analyst is *not* a poet, or a creative writer: in psychoanalysis, the subject is not aesthetics but the individual. Is the patient's formulation, once spoken to the analyst, no longer his as entirely or sufficiently as it was, like the poet's creation, now in the reader's hand? Notions of potential space and "thirdness" come to mind: for example, Winnicott's transitional object (1971), Green's analytic object (1972), and Ogden's analytic third (1994). Freud takes a respectful position in relation to the artist, and also to the patient, who in this regard occupies a role something like the poet's.

That said, there is also a clinical sense of form. We might find some similarity, for example, in the technique of Jonson's lines to the elements of an effective interpretation: the couplet is straightforward, it's compact, it's got punch—without seeming clever or showy—and it plainly emphasizes taking care to attend with the aim to understand. It says no more than necessary. Like the analytic process, the poem also reaches back to the beginning, conjoining "reader" in the title to "understand" at the end. And, like a good interpretation, the words ring true.

Form, then, is definitive: it creates limit, selecting a particular experience, enabling particular, finite meanings, from an infinite glut. First, in listening to the poem, there is the perception of beauty in what the couplet has just offered; then, or I should say, simultaneously, something is expressed. An experience comes alive kinetically in the poem; there is movement, and as that happens—as it "goes" somewhere—there is the realization that it's going to end: the poem is done, terminating with the click of the rhyme. Something has transpired, and it's over—transient. Similarly, we might say, the treatment room door closes at the end of the hour. Paradoxically, the poet's freedom of expression, and the freshness and emotional force, are possible only because of the formal arrangement: the limitation. In that profound paradox—possibility, an expanded awareness, emerging out of limitation—there is likeness to the clinical setting. The pleasure, and the transience, of the poem, of the mountain walk with friends; the fleeting beauty of the summer landscape; the power of the therapeutic conversation: each will end, and the aim is to find a particular meaning in the transitory.

In analysis too, then, the power of a form, of a structured limit, enables understanding. Not just temporal limit (the fifty-minute hour, for example) but the limitations of any human being. Every human life is transient, every person imperfect, patient and analyst alike. Every thought and feeling is transient. The clinical relevance of Freud's paper is in its focus on impermanence and limitation; on loss and mourning; on the finding of meaning; and, in that process, on making something. In "Thoughts for the Times on War and Death," written in the same period as "On Transience," Freud muses on the function of art: out of the "unbearable intensity of our grief," he writes:

> [We] seek in the world of fiction, in literature and in the theater, compensation for what has been lost in life. There we still find people who know how to die—who, indeed, even manage to kill someone else … In the realm of fiction we find the plurality of lives which we need. We die with the hero with whom we have identified ourselves; yet we survive him, and are ready to die again just as safely with another hero.
>
> (1915b: 291)

Just as safely, Freud movingly says, we are ready to die again.

The clinical setting, too, is a realm of fiction—an artifice though not artificial (any more than the child's, or a playwright's, "make-believe" is artificial). There a drama is set in motion where one desires, perhaps dies, or kills, hates or loves, safely enough. But, unlike actors or personae in a play, or characters in a story, the players in the treatment room are real. The analyst's own vulnerability—his or her merely human limitation—is part of the form: human imperfection animates the clinical work. A god won't do, a machine or a Houyhnhnm won't do. Houyhnhnms, those cool, angelic horses in Jonathan Swift's *Gulliver's Travels*, are creatures of pure reason. The rational Houyhnhnm, among other attributes, has no unconscious, harbors no self-doubt. He does not suffer and feels no guilt.

Unsure how to spell "Houyhnhnm," I turned to the Internet, where I found in that miracle, Wikipedia, the following:

> The Houyhnhnms' lack of passion surfaces mainly during their annual meeting. A visitor apologizes for being late … as her husband had just died and she had to make the proper arrangements for the funeral … She eats her lunch like all the other Houyhnhnms and is not affected at all by her loss, rationalizing that gone is gone.

There is no lingering attachment, even remotely, of a human kind. No, a perfectly rational, guilt-free Houyhnhnm won't do clinically. We die, and gone *is* gone. But clinical technique is based on imperfection: on temporal, human, cognitive, and mortal imperfection.

A Houyhnhnm-like ideal of pure rationalism comes in for criticism from Leo Stone. Stone, writing mid-century, resists the notion of strict analytic incognito: "the elements of abstinence augmenting transference intensity should derive preponderantly from the formal (i.e., explicitly technical) factors (in which I include nonresponse to primitive transference wishes) rather than from excessively rigorous deficits in human response" (1961: 69). Stone's language here is itself strikingly cold and convoluted, as if to mask his thoroughly humane outlook in Latinate, quasi-scientific terminology: he obscures the important point (almost apologetically) even as he makes it.

I agree with those who view the effort to find meaning as a process akin to mourning—Freud's "working-through." Both analyst and patient, from their different seats, are drawn into that process. Among the things to be mourned is the finitude of the relationship itself: the situation with its limits awakens longing, and desire, but stringently restricts action, on both sides. That same stringency, as we know, also fans the flame of wanting—abstinence (again) is both technical and ethical, stoking the fire and at the same time protecting against the temptation between two people to act on desire.

The clinician's task is to preserve the psychic terrain, countering the regressive pull toward omnipotence. In remaining the analyst, convinced of the *reality* of the other person, the analyst facilitates growth, his or her own as well as the patient's. As Warren Poland (2000) has written, on the function of witnessing, the analyst beholds the other "from a position of separated otherness" (21). Forty years earlier, Loewald (1980 [1960]) makes a similar point when he writes that the analyst avoids "molding the patient in the analyst's own image," a goal requiring "an objectivity and neutrality the essence of which is love and respect for the individual and for individual development" (229–230). Inevitably the effort falls short, as any human instrument must, but implicit is the analyst's striving. On striving, and on "benevolent neutrality," André Green writes:

> Benevolence is not in contradiction with neutrality; nor the latter with benevolence … Receptivity, availability, evenness of temper, no doubt form the mental configuration of an ideal analyst who only exists in

books and in the analyst's mind. And even if it is difficult for him to achieve this, at least he knows what he is striving at.

(2005: 35)

Comments such as these recall Weil's (1963) definition of love as "belief in the existence of other human beings as such" (56). Looked at that way, the analyst's interpretation—a choice to analyze, to find words that convey understanding of another person rather than to act—is a gift of the self, and a form of love.

Gone is gone, says the Houyhnhnm. But we're fortunate that Freud gives us another nuanced meditation on loss—the celebrated narrative in *Beyond the Pleasure Principle* about his toddler grandson, playing with wooden spool and string: "fort-da." With charming detachment Freud writes:

> I have been able, through a chance opportunity which presented itself, to throw some light upon the first game played by a little boy of one and a half and invented by himself. It was more than a mere fleeting observation, for I lived under the same roof as the child and his parents for some weeks, and it was some time before I discovered the meaning of the puzzling activity which he constantly repeated.
>
> (1920: 14)

In what is the first recorded psychoanalytic infant observation, Freud closely watches the child, a "good little boy" who lets his mother go without fuss. The boy repeatedly tosses his toy over the side of his cot, *fort* (gone), then pulls it back, *da* (there). Freud paints the delightful scene:

> The child had a wooden reel with a piece of string tied round it. It never occurred to him to pull it along the floor behind him, for instance, and play at its being a carriage. What he did was to hold the reel by the string and very skillfully throw it over the edge of his curtained cot, so that it disappeared into it, at the same time uttering his expressive "o-o-o-o". He then pulled the reel out of the cot again by the string and hailed its reappearance with a joyful "da" [there]. This, then, was the complete game—disappearance and return. As a rule one only witnessed its first act, which was repeated untiringly as a game in itself, though there is no doubt that the greater pleasure was attached to the

second act ... The interpretation of the game then became obvious. It was related to the child's great cultural achievement.

(Freud 1920: 15)

The game, playing "gone," says Freud, is the eighteen-month-old's "great cultural achievement." The toddler uses his imagination to make something out of his pain, giving it shape and meaning, thus organizing and tolerating an experience of loss: it is a process of mourning, and a means by which he grows. In emphasizing the untiring repetition of disappearance—the "first act"—punctuated by the toddler's spoken "o-o-o-o" (*fort*), Freud captures the centrality of language to the developmental process, a kind of magic imbued in the baby's expressiveness. Freud too makes something in writing "On Transience," confronting loss and finitude, and with his artful words he moves the reader. So too does the poet Ben Jonson with the couplet which goes "fort" to the reader and then, a little like magic, "da!" as it is understood.

There's an additional poignancy to the nursery scene: Freud first observes the child's game in 1915 but writes the narrative in 1920 when the child, his grandchild, is not quite six. The boy's mother has recently died, in January of 1920. That mother, of course, is Freud's own daughter Sophie, twenty-six years old and pregnant when she dies of influenza. Freud completes *Beyond the Pleasure Principle* later that same year. Whose imagination is at work here, overcoming pain? Who's playing "gone," whose grief are we witnessing, in the writer's description and analysis of the game? In the shadows there is something else the grandfather knows: this particular, actual child who is playing at tossing the reel/mother away will in 1920, at age five, lose that mother forever.

All development takes place against a backdrop of loss, in a giving up of omnipotence that never ends until the final loss. The little boy is learning, he doesn't own or control his mother: she is separate. The spool is the mother, gone, and then returned: "fort," then "da." She says, in effect, "I am here." But, even more important, the little boy who creates the drama is also saying "I am here": *I* did this, I'm the one who *made* it! He is like the poet, and like his essayist grandfather, working through his grief. "There are artists," writes Loewald, "for whom parting with their product is very difficult":

... much as a child is reluctant to give up a blanket or teddy bear or to share toys with other children. The journey undertaken in differentiating between subjectivity and objectivity is not an easy one—it requires differentiation not only between self and others as persons but also between self and a world of things no longer under omnipotent-magical control. When the creator's consent to this objectification is achieved to a significant degree, he is able to turn his attention to new imaginative work—having allowed such detachment to take its course.

(2000 [1988]: 511)

A similar process perhaps figures in the poet's work of completing his couplet, "To the Reader," and then letting it go.

Among Freud's (1920) rich interpretations of the child's accomplishment: he allows his mother to go away without protest, and compensates himself by "staging the disappearance and return of the objects within his reach." The boy creates a "joyful return," and then Freud adds another motive, the turning of passive to active. With comedy and delight he speaks the boy's defiance, "All right then, go away! I don't need you. I'm sending you away myself" (16). And there's another satisfaction: revenge, in throwing her away. But in this toddler's play, it's never for a moment in doubt who controls that wooden spool! The little boy is the choreographer of loss. With all of these stagings, Freud writes, the boy "work[s] over in the mind [an] overpowering experience so as to make [himself] master of it" (16). Just so, one stages scenes in analysis, working over experiences in the mind (and sometimes, like the angry, defiant child, wants to say to the needed loved one, "All right, then, go away!").

Winnicott's 1941 paper "The Observation of Infants in a Set Situation" provides, perhaps intentionally, a companion piece to Freud's description in 1920 of his young grandson. Winnicott systematically observes babies several months younger than Freud's toddler in consultation with their mothers; the babies range between five and thirteen months. Winnicott describes the clinic setting—"an instrument of research," he calls it—and, like Freud, he creates a delightful scene:

I ask the mother to sit opposite me with the angle of the table coming between me and her. She sits down with the baby on her knee. I place a right-angled shining tongue-depressor at the edge of the table and I invite the mother to place the child in such a way that, if the child should wish to handle the spatula, this is possible. Ordinarily, a mother will understand what I am about, and it is easy for me gradually to describe to her that there is to be a space of time in which she and I will contribute as little as possible to the situation, so that what happens can fairly be put down to the child's account.

(Winnicott 1941: 229–230)

"She and I will contribute as little as possible to the situation" is a little like analytic abstinence, conveying an attitude, and a holding back, which sets things in motion. The regulated clinic setting includes two calmly detached, seated observers (one of them a stranger to the baby) and a shiny object (an "instrument"); a drama, created by the infant, then slowly takes shape. Attracted to the object but at first anxiously hesitant to reach for it, the baby "gradually becomes brave enough to let his feelings develop." The writer Winnicott is playful, the scene is amusing:

> The moment at which this first phase changes into the second is evident, for the child's acceptance of the reality of desire for the spatula is heralded by a change in the inside of the mouth, which becomes flabby, while the tongue looks thick and soft, and saliva flows copiously. Before long he puts the spatula into his mouth and is chewing it with his gums, or seems to be copying father smoking a pipe. The change in the baby's behaviour is a striking feature. Instead of expectancy and stillness there now develops self-confidence …

(Winnicott 1941: 231)

The "phases" Winnicott identifies are like sequential play scenes; and soon, as with Freud's toddler, there's little doubt who controls the shiny object:

> The baby now seems to feel that the spatula is in his possession, perhaps in his power, certainly available for the purposes of self-expression. He bangs with it on the table or on a metal bowl which is nearby on the table, making as much noise as he can; or else he holds it to my mouth and to his mother's mouth, very pleased if we pretend to be fed by it. He definitely wishes us to play at being fed, and is upset if we should be so stupid as to take the thing into our mouths and spoil the game as a game … At this point, I might mention that I have never

seen any evidence of a baby being disappointed that the spatula is, in fact, neither food nor a container of food.

(Winnicott 1941: 231)

That is, the baby fully understands the artifice and says, in effect, "Let's pretend!" Winnicott (1941) parenthetically notes: "In passing, I would mention the fact that I find therapeutic work can be done in this (set) situation" (231). Though no words are spoken, something beneficial to the baby is accomplished in the process.

Winnicott then likens the structured observation of infants to the adult analytic setting, where language is the central medium of exchange; he speaks directly to the patient's possessiveness and desire: "Each interpretation," Winnicott (1941) writes, "is a glittering object which excites the patient's greed" (246). Although he tends to leave out of his descriptions of both settings, infant and adult, any explicit reference to the analyst— the living presence who offers the spatula, or makes the interpretation— the analogy of course extends to include the analyst herself as glittering object of excitement and desire. The comedy of Winnicott's rendition invites imagining the shiny object in the patient's "possession," and the many ways, loving and hating, tender and violent, the patient might, with increasing freedom and pleasure, wield that human instrument for "purposes of self-expression."

Winnicott's spatula brings to mind another of Leo Stone's remarks caricaturing the stance of the so-called "classical" analyst: "The enthusiastic and engaging assertion of an older colleague many years ago that his patient would have developed the same vivid transference love toward him 'if he had been a brass monkey,'" writes Stone (1961), "is alas (or perhaps fortunately!) just not true" (41). On such an understanding, the analyst is merely robotic—a nominal, interchangeable mechanism, more a disembodied abstraction, than a real person. In the spirit of Winnicott's desirous salivating playful baby, the analysand might retort: "It may be a brass monkey, but it's *my* brass monkey!"

Later in the paper Winnicott refers directly to Freud's little boy who throws away the cotton reel, and he extends Freud's thinking:

[W]hen the mother goes away, this is not only a loss for him of the externally real mother but also a test of his relation to his inside mother. This inside [or, internal] mother to a large extent reflects his own feelings, and may be loving or terrifying, or changing rapidly from one attitude to the other. When he finds he can master his relation to his inside mother, including his aggressive riddance of her (Freud brings this out clearly), he can allow the disappearance of his external mother, and not too greatly fear her return.

(Winnicott 1941: 247)

Reading Winnicott's sentences, one can't but hear in the background the toddler's joyful "Da!".

"The child's great cultural achievement" suggests a concept of art as reparation, as well as reunification. Loewald (2000 [1988]) asks: "Could sublimation be both a mourning of lost original oneness, and a celebration of oneness regained?" (517).[2] Eighty years earlier, in "Creative Writers and Day-Dreaming," Freud (1908) explores the underlying dynamics within the individual out of which comes a creation. Already thinking about the function of play, there he writes (actually, he exclaims): "If we could at least discover in ourselves or in people like ourselves an activity which was in some way akin to creative writing!" (143). If we could find such an activity, it wouldn't make all of us into writers (or into great poets), but examining it, Freud says, might help us understand what writers are about. Note the direction he takes, looking back in time at the commonplace, the ordinary:

> Should we not look for the first traces of imaginative activity as early as in childhood? The child's best-loved and most intense occupation is with his play or games. Might we not say that every child at play behaves like a creative writer, in that he creates a world of his own, or, rather, re-arranges the things of his world in a new way which pleases him? It would be wrong to think he does not take that world seriously; on the contrary, he takes his play very seriously and he expends large amounts of emotion on it. *The opposite of play is not what is serious but what is real.*
>
> (Freud 1908: 143–144, emphasis added)

The writer does the same as the child at play. Both create an imaginary world and take it seriously; both borrow from the world, and rearrange it for pleasure. Is there a difference? Grown-ups don't go on playing like children. "Actually," in one of Freud's (1908) famous remarks, "we can never give anything up; we only exchange one thing for another" (145). The grown-up doesn't give up the child's pleasure but instead introduces a change: "What appears to be a renunciation," he writes, "is really the formation of a substitute or surrogate" (145).

Implicit in this idea of play, and substitution, is the concept of form. On the subject of form, the critic Francis Fergusson writes, in his *The Idea of a Theater*, "The soul of the cat is the form of its body":

> Kittens, in their play, seem to be using something like our histrionic sensibility. They directly perceive each other's actions: stalking an imagined quarry; the bluff and formal defiance which precedes a fight; flight in terror; the sudden indifference which ends the play ... When the kittens are only playing, their perception and imitation of action resembles art: they seem to enjoy something like the pleasure of the contemplation of form; and the actions of hunting or defiance more rhythmic or harmonious than those of real hunting or fighting, approach the ceremonial disinterestedness of the hunting-dance or the war-dance.
>
> (Fergusson 1949: 237)

Ceremony, like daydreaming, or like theater, is an adult version of play. In Freud's (1908) words, "Instead of playing, [the grown-up] now phantasies. He builds castles in the air and creates what are called daydreams" (145); the adult, that is, imagines—perhaps another form or manifestation of the process of mourning. "[E]very single phantasy," writes Freud, "is the fulfillment of a wish, a correction of unsatisfying reality" (146).

Just so, the kittens' actions, "more rhythmic or harmonious than those of real hunting or fighting," are an improvement over a wanting reality, as well as a form of practice for the real hunt (or the actual fight). Freud's interest, to note again, is *psychoanalytic*. He is focused on the nature of the subject (the writer's process) more than on the value of the object (the work of art). Freud (1916b) of course does appreciate the value of the writer's art, elsewhere—perhaps nowhere more directly than in "The Exceptions," when he notes the "subtle economy of art in the poet" (315). As I have suggested earlier (see Chapter 3), there may be an analogy between the poet's (or writer's) art and the therapeutic principle of abstinence. That idea can be extended, cautiously, to the analyst's interpretive skill.

But here Freud is exploring a different kind of universal: the underlying dynamics that enable imaginative work. He is proposing that all people— children, adults, writers—have phantasies with which they defend themselves against unsatisfactory reality. (I stay with the Strachey translation and spelling of "phantasy"; for an account of the distinction between the two words, Freudian vs. Kleinian "phantasy," and "fantasy," see Spillius [2001]). That reality is unsatisfactory is for Freud a given. And to play on that reality, to compensate for it, and transform it—to phantasize—is in the nature of human beings. One sees here a connection to the toddler's game, and to a grieving process: in compensating for the loss of mother, the boy transforms the unhappy reality, fashioning it to his liking.

Briefly, the process Freud (1908) describes goes something like this: a current event rouses a desire, and "[f]rom there it harks back to a memory of an earlier experience … in which this wish was fulfilled" (147). In this way, present and past are brought together, and the phantasy, or daydream (or the child's play) yields a future—the three moments of time thus unified. In Freud's (1908) memorable words, musical even in translation: "Thus past, present and future are strung together, as it were, on the thread of the wish that runs through them" (148). (The German reads: *Also Vergangenes, Gegenwärtiges, Zukünftiges wie an der Schnur des durchlaufenden Wunsches aneinandergereiht*.) Like dreams (though also differently from dreams), phantasies are wish fulfillments, reviving infantile impressions while evading censorship. Phantasy distorts memory in order to conceal it: it is as paradoxical as the transference, Freud's clearly related preoccupation. Phantasying performs the functions both of resistance and access, closing and opening—like the analytic transference, both covering and exposing.

Freud (1908) focuses mainly on mediocre authors in "Creative Writers and Day-Dreaming"—those who lack "art" (writers of romances, potboilers, forms of escapist fiction)—because his subject is the universal function of phantasying in the cultural endeavor. Implicit, however, is his fascination with poetic art and the pleasure given: "How the writer accomplishes this is his innermost secret" (153), Freud writes (perhaps somewhat disingenuously). How does the artist touch us? In contrast to the ordinary daydreamer, "[t]he writer softens the character of his egoistic daydreams by altering and disguising it, and he bribes us by the purely formal—that is, aesthetic—yield of pleasure which he offers us in the presentation of his phantasies" (153). Reading Freud's words, perhaps one hears again the pleasing sound of Ben Jonson's short poem. Some authors are more truth-evading than truth-seeking; but phantasy accommodates both evading and seeking, in different proportion (again, like the transference).

With the notion of evading and seeking, there is another likeness to the richness of the toddler's *fort/da* game: forth and back, back and forth; lost and found, gone and returned; destroy and retrieve, hide-and-seek—played over and over again. Seated unseen behind the couch, the analyst too is both present and absent, seen and not seen, both found and lost, over and over. Much later, Winnicott will write, in his profound paper "Communicating and Not Communicating Leading to a Study of Certain Opposites": "At the center of each person is an incommunicado element, and this is sacred." Winnicott (1963) poses the question: "how to be isolated without having to be insulated?" and he ties the "hard fact" of the individual as a permanent isolate to the softening effect of the "sharing that belongs to the whole range of cultural experience" (187). The relevance to Freud's thinking about play and the imagination in 1908 is clear. "It is a sophisticated game of hide-and-seek," Winnicott also writes, "in which it is joy to be hidden but disaster not to be found" (186). A similar ambiguity, or oscillation, characterizes the clinical exchange.

I have described the psychoanalytic situation as "an intimacy that intends separation": the work begins, the work will end.[3] The carefully structured arrangement offers an extraordinary freedom within constraint—a "yes," you may speak freely but also a "no," we will not touch. The intention is to understand, served by a repeated come close, then part; speak desire, don't touch: "yes" coupled with a "no." The odd arrangement is also fiduciary, based on trust: one person pays the other for an allotment of time, attention, and trustworthiness. We're in the marketplace, a purchase is made. As in Jonson's poem, the aim "to understand" depends upon a disciplined formality, a finitude that enacts content. And there's also a plainness: the boundary is as distinct, as absolute as, for example, the way the verbal sounds of "hand" and "understand" in Jonson's poem are alike and unlike. The meanings the form enables may feel infinite, but the formal aperture to them is clearly *de*limited. The intensity and the richness of conviction about what's "true" is informed by the particular and finite.

If the analysis of Jonson's "To the Reader" illuminates some elements of a literary instrument, and Winnicott informs us about the "set situation" as an observational instrument in relation to babies, what in the analytic situation comprises the *clinical* instrument? How does the analyst's work *work*? Its force is suggested by those four words Freud invokes early in "On Transience": scarcity value in time. Scarcity too is a form of finitude. The poet in Freud's narrative feels no joy in the landscape, he's despondent at the fleeting nature of beauty. Just as he does in the narrative about his grandson's play, Freud engages the reader with immediacy, creating a vivid scene. The language is full of melody:

> Not long ago I went on a summer walk through a smiling countryside in the company of a taciturn friend and of a young but already famous poet. The poet admired the beauty of the scene around us but felt no joy in it. He was disturbed by the thought that all this beauty was fated to extinction, that it would vanish when winter came, like all human beauty and all the beauty and splendour that men have created or may create. All that he would otherwise have loved and admired seemed to him to be shorn of its worth by the transience which was its doom.
>
> (Freud 1916a: 306)

Freud (1916a) won't dispute that all things are transient, nor can he "insist upon an exception in favour of what is beautiful and perfect. But," he retorts, "I did dispute the poet's pessimistic view that the transience of what is beautiful involves any loss in its worth. On the contrary," he exclaims, "an increase! *Transience value is scarcity value in time.* Limitation in the possibility of an enjoyment," he writes, "raises the value of the enjoyment" (306, emphasis added). Value: we're back in the marketplace—scarcity has benefits; when supply is limited, worth increases.

As a way of relating Freud's striking statement to the clinical situation, I'll return to a personal example of a particular loss: someone's transience. My own analyst died suddenly.[4] Someone who mattered—not family, not friend—was gone. There was a felt intensity to the loss, with a range of feelings, from anger to sorrow to (even) relief, but it was not the same as losing someone close in my "real" life, outside the treatment room. A significant loss, but also peculiar, at best. Whom, and *what*, exactly, had I lost? What had I paid for, what had I received? The clinical situation aims to stir intensity, an outsized magnitude in the attachment to a human being suddenly gone. How could I grieve if I didn't quite know who was gone and what I was grieving (much less whom to grieve with)?

All of these questions, it seems to me, have profound clinical relevance for every psychoanalytic treatment, and for every ending, whether problematic or relatively routine. They are questions of definition and of finite limitations. And all arose from a particular, and distinctly psychoanalytic, transience.

When I call the psychoanalytic situation an intimacy that intends separation, I mean, among many other things, the power of the work for both people, though the roles differ: an emotional intensity—we name it the transference and the countertransference—created by the forms of limitation, or the limits imposed by form. In addition to temporal limit, the form includes, for the analyst, a special kind of limiting detachment, remote yet close; for the patient, it includes uncensored speech, a new, raw, uncloaked form of expression. There are few ordinary social niceties, on either side of the couch: a formal requirement, one might even say, to be uncivil. It's not natural! Gone is any illusion of one's grown-up propriety—perhaps another loss to be mourned.

The analytic situation is also structured to enforce a recurring kind of loss that may take many forms: the hour ends, Friday comes; or, an interpretation, which confronts one with words rather than the "wished-for." Interpretation (Winnicott's glittering object of desire) is an instrument for evasion and at the same time the essential business of communication— another paradox, and another form of incivility. The patient gets hold of something, or retrieves a closeness, an emotional intensity and, whoosh, in a reiterated "yes-no," it's interrupted—gone. Intensity is created, for both partners, by the intimacies and exclusions imposed by form. Scarcity is an instrument of the external (the set-up, the frame, the analyst's abstinent stance and carefully spoken words), but it's *instrumental* in exciting all kinds of things in the psyche.

That intense excitement, coupled with loss, increases both worth and power, which is to say, exactly, "scarcity value in time": day after day, things one has are gone, "da" and "fort." No wonder one gets angry! Winnicott, writing about infant aggression when the mother goes away, says that the child then tests the relation to the "inside mother." Years later he playfully expresses the same idea of loss followed by retrieval in "The Use of an Object":

The subject says to the object: "I destroyed you", and the object is there to receive the communication. From now on the subject says:

"Hullo object!" "I destroyed you." "I love you." "You have value for me because of your survival of my destruction of you."

(Winnicott 1969: 713)

"Fort-da," the patient says as subject. "I threw *you* out; and here you are. You have value. I love you." Pursuing a similar idea, but reversing things, with reunion followed by new loss, André Green notes Winnicott's different formulation of that inversion:

[T]he end of every session [according to Winnicott] had to be considered, from the patient's standpoint, as the repetition of a rejection by the primary object. In short each session is experienced repeating a process of reunion-separation, the latter arriving after an attempt at reunion ...

(Green 2005: 34)

"Da-fort," the time is up, you have to go. The psychoanalytic situation is purposefully structured to enforce *practicing* that reality.

But the "gone/not gone" in the treatment room, day after day, is more expected than shocking. The regular exposure to loss under bearable, formalized conditions fortifies the patient, helps her acknowledge, and transform, the real losses, and lets her practice for the more extreme, less expected losses life outside the treatment room inevitably brings. With a loss, enacted over and over—its meaning plumbed for both patient and analyst, though for the latter that work is kept more private—the analyst's offering, I believe, increases in value.

I've tried to present the essence: the creation of value in the psychoanalytic situation by means of scarcity. But perhaps the picture I've painted is too rosy. The forces stirred between the two people in the treatment room can have unruly power. How does one allow for such intensity, deliberately firing up the emotional cauldron, with the goal of serving the patient's well-being, and at the same time enable both people to tolerate the heat? Danger is implicit: the psychoanalytic project by its nature is always threatened—and threatening. The analyst offers a mortal gift— "mortal" not just in the sense of a human gift: the offering is also fragile, and can be corrupted.

The psychoanalytic transference is at the center of the clinical process. In a way, similar to the analyst's interpretation, the transference is not only the essential vehicle for the work of analysis, it is also an evasion. More than fifty years ago, Thomas Szasz (1963), a controversial, even oppositional figure (viewed by some at the time as an enemy of psychoanalysis), wrote: "Transference is the pivot upon which the entire structure of psycho-analytic treatment rests" (443); at the same time, he adds, it serves as a defense to protect the analyst, carrying the potential for misunderstanding, misuse, and exploitation:

> [I]f the patient loves or hates the analyst, and if the analyst can view these attitudes as transferences, then, in effect, the analyst has convinced himself that the patient does not have these feelings and dispositions towards him. The patient does not really love or hate the analyst, but someone else. What could be more reassuring?
>
> (Szasz 1963: 437–438)

And, with the acute perception sometimes attained by an enemy, Szasz writes:

> On the one hand, [the concept of transference] enabled the analyst to work where he could not otherwise have worked; on the other, it exposed him to the danger of being "wrong" vis-à-vis his patient— and of abusing the analytic relationship—without anyone being able to demonstrate this to him … It is an inspired and indispensable concept; yet it also harbours the seeds, not only of its own destruction, but of the destruction of psycho-analysis itself. Why? Because it tends to place the person of the analyst beyond the reality testing of patients, colleagues, and self. This hazard must be frankly recognized.
>
> (Szasz 1963: 442–443)

This "hazard" returns us to the opening question of this chapter: how can these two people, so deeply attached within the odd intimate form, separate? Within that form, how can they say goodbye? Does the situation invite trouble, as in Goethe's "The Sorcerer's Apprentice," by setting in motion a process liable to spiral out of control? Is the analyst/interpreter inevitably an arbiter of the patient's experience? On the benign end of a range, the analyst strives neither to mold the patient according to his idea of what the patient should become (Loewald) nor does he intrude destructively (Winnicott); on the malignant end, he is an erring judge, and exploits the analytic relationship without, in Szasz's words, "anyone being able to demonstrate this to him." Winnicott's hyperbolic remark about the potential "threat to the isolated core" captures with comic genius the dangers of the psychoanalytic situation, drawing attention to the very real power the analyst has to misuse the patient. Outrageously, provocatively, mischievously, Winnicott states:

> Rape, and being eaten by cannibals, these are mere bagatelles as compared with the violation of the self's core, the alteration of the self's central elements by communication seeping through the defenses. For me this would be the sin against the self. We can understand the hatred people have of psycho-analysis which has penetrated a long way into the human personality, and which provides a threat to the human individual in his need to be secretly isolated.
>
> (Winnicott 1963: 187)

I've quoted Winnicott, Hans Loewald, Leo Stone, and the perceptive curmudgeon-outcast Thomas Szasz—all four mid-century figures writing in a period when much about psychoanalysis is being reconsidered. Psychoanalysis is at the peak of its centrality in the culture. And at the same time ferment is bubbling.

The period also presents some bizarre but revealing attempts to deal with the discipline's formal rigidities as well as its troubling paradoxes and dilemmas. In 1968, for example, an odd paper appeared in the psychoanalytic literature: Lawrence Kubie's "Unsolved Problems in the Resolution of the Transference." Kubie, a central, respected figure in the psychoanalytic world—a charismatic presence who himself enjoyed, perhaps even flourished, on controversy—tries to address a specific problem that has struck him over his decades-long clinical experience: the difficulty of bringing treatment to a satisfactory conclusion. Once set in motion, how does the psychoanalytic process end? Within the intimate form, dual and imbalanced, how do the two people say goodbye? "I have been impressed," Kubie writes:

> by many observations of how transference processes which had been essential for both the exploratory and therapeutic progress of the analysis could toward the end seem to turn upon the analytic process and destroy it. This led me to ask whether the therapist who conducts the

treatment is the one man who cannot terminate it, and whether the technical principles which are essential for the progress of treatment obstruct its conclusion.

(Kubie 1968: 331)

Here Kubie, the eminent insider, as though hyper-extending the outsider Szasz's notion of the transference paradox, suggests that transference, the essential instrument of an analysis, at the same time also carries the potential for its destruction. "[I]t is possible," he writes further, "that the more intense and creative the transference relationship during the treatment, the more dangerous may be its rupture at the termination of treatment" (1968: 347–348). Kubie reaches for a pragmatic solution, his suggestion inadvertently belittling the capacities of both analyst and patient: I mean, in the analyst, qualities such as technical skill, humanity, and integrity; and, in the patient, the capacity as well as the right to work through the intense and rich transference relationship he, or she, has created. Kubie speculates whether "[the] substitution of one analyst for another had made it easier to resolve the tangled skein of the transference without the desperate intensification that tends so frequently to occur toward the end of treatment" (332). This notion of a substitute is a little like bringing in a new pitcher to finish the baseball game—the "closer."

Kubie's paper, with its unlikely (though apparently serious) suggestion of a relief-analyst for termination, is symptomatic: does it sound a note of desperation? Rupture, in this scenario, is managed by introducing further rupture. "Rupture" itself is a strikingly violent word for concluding the therapeutic relationship. (In another way, so is the technical word, "termination.") I have tried to illuminate the clinical relevance of "scarcity value" in understanding the therapeutic arrangement as a structured limitation that enables possibility, depth of attachment, and healing. Kubie's implausible solution to a problem inherent in the transference instrument is to remove the companion. Scarcity here is countered, on the one hand, by a weird duplicative abundance (give the patient another analyst/brass-monkey) and, on the other, by a wrenching deprivation, escalating that "scarcity" to an absolute.

I began this chapter with the idea that form is definitive, fostering expanded awareness and growth. It's perhaps no exaggeration to say that Kubie's proposition, by disrupting the dyad, violently dismantles the psychoanalytic form—which is a process of working-through. If one cannot (or refuses to) mourn, Freud (1914a) reminds us in "On Transience," one is afraid to love. "[I]n the last resort," he also writes (in "On Narcissism"), "we must begin to love in order not to fall ill, and we are bound to fall ill if, in consequence of frustration, we are unable to love" (85). Whose is the failure here, who is afraid to love? John Klauber remarks on the strains inherent to being an analyst:

> Practically no word ever appears in the literature about how the analyst manages to form relationship after relationship of the most intimate kind with patient after patient, of the mourning that he must feel for each one of them, and of how he discharges it.
>
> (Klauber 1981: 174)

Mourning is at the center of the termination process, for both people in the treatment room. In a defensive denial, Kubie proposes closing down that process, where the workings of grief and love inevitably entwine. Hardening himself to loss, both his own and the patient's, the analyst is more vulnerable to misjudgment, possibly even to ethical lapse. I think again of Dr. O, whose defensive gesture of "not intruding" I have earlier described as "an upside-down breach of the analytic frame: he is not too loose but instead too tight and unbending" (see Chapter 3).

Finally, and remarkably, Kubie claims that the analyst's performance is perfectly "correct," and beyond reproach. The termination trouble, he writes,

> has nothing to do with the skill of the initial therapist. It has only to do with the patient's ambivalent need for and fear of the resolution of a relationship whose very intensity was essential for the progress of therapy but at the same time made the ending of it so upsetting as to threaten everything that had been gained.
>
> (Kubie 1968: 437)

Thus, Kubie offers the taxed and possibly anxious clinician a sedative: or, to put it differently, a convenient escape, implicitly blaming the patient not only for the inevitable stresses of ending but for the looming destruction of the *entire prolonged investment* in the analysis—an extraordinary statement. (One perhaps hears an echo of Winnicott: the analyst's retaliation is worse than death—or even his hyperbolic remark, "violation of the self's core.") Kubie's (1968) tone in such passages is not only complacent but blandly superior: "Many patients are gifted human beings of quality and worth," he writes (344–345).

This measured calm—a rationalistic extreme—calls to mind the lady Houyhnhnm who comes late to a meeting, having just made funeral arrangements ("proper" ones) for her husband, and eats her lunch like all the other Houyhnhnms, unaffected by her loss: gone, after all, is merely gone. The image of a "closer" analyst does make one laugh, perhaps in the way a New Yorker "couch" cartoon might; and, at the same time, if taken seriously, in its implications for both patient and analyst, Kubie's presentation of his notion is heartbreaking. Later generations of psychoanalysts will continue to work at finding calming explanations, and rationalizations, with a variety of defining metaphors, for this complex and hazardous arrangement, the psychoanalytic situation. Is the analyst a mirror? A repository? A guide? A witness? A shield? A lamp? A fellow traveler? How many images must be invoked in order to understand, and effectively manage, the analytic offering? In Chapter 5, I turn to explore such questions.

I'll close this chapter by returning to poetry. Alice Jones (2013) quotes Dan Chiasson's description of Shakespeare's sonnets as like "little contraptions designed to stop, and yet unable to stop, the passing of time" (2008: 82). This little contraption—"On Transience"—the gorgeous piece of writing I'm considering here, gives us a man of sorrow. Perhaps Freud even foresees the transience of psychoanalysis itself. Will the discipline perish? Like a Shakespearean sonnet, this brief essay is a device that would stop time, yet be unable to stop the passing of time. If Freud struggled with grief and mourning, as we all must (unless we're a Houyhnhnm), then we might better appreciate his most ingenious creation—the psychoanalytic situation itself—as a little contraption for transforming sorrow, working through griefs, creating something new.

Here is a sonnet more recent than Shakespeare: Sonnet 5, from *Clearances* by Seamus Heaney, subtitled "In Memoriam, M. K. H., 1911–1984." The poem's M. K. H. is Heaney's mother:

Sonnet 5
The cool that came off sheets just off the line
Made me think the damp must still be in them
But when I took my corners of the linen
And pulled against her, first straight down the hem

And then diagonally, then flapped and shook
The fabric like a sail in a cross-wind,
They made a dried-out undulating thwack.
So we'd stretch and fold and end up hand to hand
For a split second as if nothing had happened
For nothing had that had not always happened
Beforehand, day by day, just touch and go,
Coming close again by holding back
In moves where I was x and she was o
Inscribed in sheets she'd sewn from ripped-out flour sacks.

"[A] dried-out undulating thwack." That's maybe a little like when the analyst delivers an especially penetrating time-stopping interpretation: an undulating *thwack*. Capturing rhythmical wave-like motion, and sound, it's like hands clapping: a punctuation point in the rhythm of recurrence in a dance of coming together and parting. And then, the dance continues— son and lost mother, writer and reader, patient and analyst.

In memory of Richard Gottlieb, 1943–2017.

Notes

1 An early version of this text was presented as part of the panel "Three Analysts on the Clinical Relevance of Freud's 'On Transience,'" at Boston Psychoanalytic Society and Institute, April 25, 2015.
2 It is not my purpose to examine the extensive literature on sublimation, though the concept's relevance is, I hope, clear.
3 See Pinsky (2002, 2012, 2014a).
4 See Introduction, this volume. See also Pinsky (2014a).

Chapter 5

Mirrors and Monsters[1]

"[T]he vile smell of the sea-fed brutes was peculiarly trying, and I should like to know who would choose a monster of the deep for bed-fellow."

—Menelaus lying in wait among the seals for Proteus
(*The Odyssey*, Book IV)

[A]bove all, please don't confuse monsters with demons. Monsters should be approached with tenderness and fond appreciation. A monster is a solitary representative of an endangered species.

—Friedman 2006: 690–691

In the previous chapter, "The Instrument," I pose a question: "Is the picture I've painted too rosy?" There, emphasizing ritual and form, I had likened the psychoanalytic process—Freud's "working-through"—to poems, to a dance, to a child's imaginative play and other creative acts. But is the best likeness, truly, to a beautiful poem by Seamus Heaney, or a couplet by Ben Jonson? Possibly a better resemblance is to something more strange, fantastical, even monstrous.

In our cultural or professional imagination, what is an analyst? What is the job, and what responsibilities come with it? How do we measure the fulfillment of those responsibilities, or their failure? I am concerned in this book with the mortality of the analyst and the profession's dilemmas in addressing it. In terms of that enterprise, what precisely—or metaphorically—does the patient lose when the analyst dies? Freud's "no model" offers little for us to envision: the analyst's course is not like anything else known. Or, from another angle, that role is like numberless different things. The protean quality is part of the point: in taking all shapes—in the infinite variety of the imagined *other*—the analyst, in the end, is also none of these. He is "only the analyst doing analysis. There *is* no model for the analyst in real life" (Hoffer 1993: 344).

On the cover of this book is the image of a plate. "Until you see it," writes the art critic Sebastian Smee (2015), "you can't begin to grasp the beauty of the colors in this mid-16th-century dish." Made in Turkey during the Ottoman period, the dish is attributed to Shahquli. Today Shahquli's style, Smee tells us, is called the "saz" style, "a reference to the stylized serrated-edge leaves he favored, often paired with Chinese dragons, phoenixes, and other mythical creatures … No fantastical creatures appear here," concludes Smee, "but the dish could hardly feel more alive" (G3).

The striking image of the plate, with its dragon shapes and saw-bladed, serpentine leaves and leonine flowers, recalls again the Gorgon Medusa reflected in the shield of the hero Perseus. I have described that mythological object, likening it to the psychoanalytic transference: a shield that is also a mirror, its protective, image-containing surface held by the young combatant (see Chapter 1). An enchanted glass, the shield enables Perseus to overcome the Gorgon without looking directly at the snakey-haired monster. Safe-kept by the analyst, the process is a clear mirror and a reliable protection, and the hero, I note there, is clearly the patient.

"Transference" is a technical expression invented to make treatment possible. A normative term in the professional vocabulary, transference is the animating process underlying treatment and, at the same time, it is a weird fantastical creature: the analyst becomes a magnet for the patient's intensity of feeling, the object of archaic love, dread, and desire. Our mind's eye can see living dragons and lions in the mythological hero's reflective shield. So too in the evocative design of the plate, or in the psychoanalytic transference, we imagine what is present figuratively, conjuring what is emotionally real for the hero-patient: the imaginative process as a constructed means of seeing reality. A more recent, corresponding creature—or, reciprocally animating co-monster (a mirror image?)—is the analyst's countertransference.

The purpose of analytic terms, as psychoanalysis was discovered (or invented), as Lawrence Friedman (2006) wryly states, "was to dress the scaly monster in a business suit." Friedman's aim, in avoiding technical language and using, as he puts it, "normal terms"—or call them commonplace words—is "to show how unnatural the monster is … [and] to light up the early unnaturalness of psychoanalytic treatment and its subsequent normalization" (691).

What Friedman does with the image of the monster forced into a business suit helps define my intention here: I think that the odd, maybe even monstrous early terms, including concepts, say, such as *abstinence* and *neutrality*, may constitute an essential vocabulary of now-endangered creatures. These old terms—Freud's guidelines and first principles—no matter how ungainly, imperfect, and endlessly caricatured, may deserve revivifying. More recent language and images in psychoanalytic writing, it seems to me, can sometimes tame or even sentimentalize the procedure, diminishing the benign monster.

Or, worse, in arrogating the heroic role for the analyst himself, the clinician, armed with protective jargon, moves to the center and becomes the protagonist. Freud's metaphors and similes—the cold mirror, the feelingless surgeon—can certainly be considered, if not monstrous, at least unfeeling. But in its minimal, cautious quality, resisting the grandiose, that original terminology may be welcome in a realm of unruly dragons, lions, and other fantastical creatures. The mirror suggests truth, and the emotionless surgeon respects mortality. Both figurative terms, in their very coolness, perhaps manifest humility, and respect for the patient.

In a traditional definition, what distinguishes us from gods and from beasts (as well as from mythological monsters) is that we know we are mortal—that adjective rich in meanings. The ultimate metonymy for humanity is an actual death; and the particular situation of the therapist's death serves here as vehicle for better understanding not only who the therapist is—that is, who he or she is beyond an ordinary human being— but also for examining the therapeutic endeavor. By means of that vehicle we may observe and usefully clarify the field of theoretical differences as well.

The psychoanalytic relationship is described as unique, repeatedly so, by analytic theorists of all stripes. Just how unusual is it? For a specific example, Ana-Maria Rizzuto (1995) plainly asserts that the patient has "never spoken to another person in such a way" (4). While it is of course a truism that the therapeutic relationship is not exactly like any other, the same can also be said of many kinds of relationship (see Chapter 3). But we don't find education experts (for example) regularly reminding us of the uniqueness of the teacher-student bond, nor do we hear much fuss over defining and redefining the essential role of the teacher. Yet that relationship too is unique, the teacher, like the therapist, in a position of trust. However, a problem of some magnitude arises if, in the articulation of what is unique to the therapeutic relationship, its likeness to other important relationships is denied, obscured, or forgotten. How are we to understand the analyst's persistent discomfort? What are the strains, what the dangers, and why is the enterprise worth it?

My project has been to place the lens of the therapist's death over the therapeutic relationship and see what is revealed by looking through it. Among other things, we need to elucidate differences from other intimate relationships, along with the inevitable similarities—despite Freud's "no model" formulation. To serve that good, I will look, in particular, at several metaphors and similes adduced over the years to conceptualize the analytic relationship and the person and function of the analyst. Considering the loss in relation to figurative language may illuminate not only the profession's neglect of the analyst's mortality and the more recent growing interest in that topic, but may also shed light on the analytic offering itself, in its nature as a mortal gift.

I'll begin at an extreme: a comically reductive metaphor. In a groundbreaking study—remarkably, the first ever to explore systematically the patient's reactions to the therapist's death—Lord, Ritvo, and Solnit (1978) report a broad range of mourning reactions in twenty-seven participants whose analysts had died. Two of the respondents appear to have experienced no mourning reaction at all following the loss. One of these, a young candidate in psychoanalytic training, is quoted as claiming that "the analyst only mattered as a transference figure … a peg on which to hang attitudes" (193).

The metaphor of the peg suggests that with the death, nothing of significance was lost: presumably one peg may be replaced with another. Why is the example absurd? Simply, because it implies that there are not two people in the treatment room—the second person is not present in human form. How much easier it is to feel no grief for the loss of a piece of wood than for the loss of a human being. The candidate's "peg" has even fewer distinguishing features than the brass monkey of Leo Stone's anecdote (quoted in Chapter 4). One particular brass monkey may not be so easily substituted for another as one featureless wooden peg for another.

Stone's colleague speaks tongue-in-cheek about the brass monkey, aiming to make the point that the patient, if engaged in the process, will necessarily develop intense feelings for the analyst, whoever he or she may be. How much those feelings will be the same, as the anecdote seems to suggest, regardless of the particular characteristics of the clinician, is something theorists still question. Correspondingly, and in addition, how do we think about the analyst's emotional experience, the countertransference—that reflection or obverse of transference? The history of the discipline's puzzlement over the nature of the engagement is lengthy, with an uneasiness already apparent in Freud's *Papers on Technique* (1911–1915). To this day analysts continue to struggle in search of adequate vocabulary for what transpires in the treatment room, not only between the two people but, subjectively, within each person. To pose a fundamental question that has woven itself through the literature (and its figurative language) for over a century: Who, or what, is the other person in the room, and in what ways is he (or she) actual or real? Phrased another way: To what purpose, and *how*, is the analyst emotionally involved, and in what ways is this experienced by the patient?

For example, Irwin Hoffman (1983), more than thirty years ago in his paper "The Patient as Interpreter of the Analyst's Experience," approaches the question by insisting on the resilience of the blank screen concept, "the idea that the analyst is not accurately perceived by the patient as a real person, but that he serves rather as a screen or mirror to whom various attitudes, feelings, and motives can be attributed" (389). The resilience of the idea is manifested, Hoffman suggests, in the vigor of the continuing protests against it (390), and I would agree. Hoffman sees the blank screen image as only one example of what he terms "asocial conceptions of the patient's experience" (390–391). Another question emerges here: What precisely is so *frightening* to the analyst about being conceived as real, as present and emotionally involved?

Two years later, coming from the British-Kleinian tradition, Irma Brenman Pick, in her rich paper "Working Through in the Countertransference" (1985), explores in plain-spoken language—more colloquially figurative than flamboyantly metaphorical—the complexity of the clinical interaction: the analyst in her account is no non-reactive blank screen.[2] Pick elaborates James Strachey's (1934) idea set forth at the end of his classic paper "The Nature of the Therapeutic Action of Psychoanalysis," that a transference interpretation (Strachey's term is "mutative interpretation," directed to "the point of urgency" [286]) is exactly what the analyst would seem to avoid: "there is sometimes a lurking difficulty in the actual *giving* of the interpretation," writes Strachey, "for there seems to be a constant temptation for the analyst to do something else instead," as if the analyst "is exposing himself to some great danger in doing so" (290–291). (The reader notes the refrain: there is danger in the treatment room.) Extending Strachey's implication, as Pick (1985) paraphrases it, "that the full or deep transference experience is disturbing to the analyst, that which the analyst most fears and wishes to avoid" (157), Pick emphasizes the clinician's own difficult but necessary internal work—the analyst, she writes, "walking the tightrope between experiencing disturbance and responding with interpretation that does not convey disturbing anxiety" (157).

Pick's tightrope image is, in a limited way, quite dramatic—the analyst envisioned as aerial acrobat; but at the same time the expression is so familiar and temperate as to become almost abstract. (I think of other timeworn figurative expressions with a similar quality: one is "juggling" a lot of appointments, for example, or "skating on thin ice.") Analyst and patient alike, Pick (1985) tells us, would wish to "eliminate discomfort as well as to communicate and share experience: these are ordinary human reactions. In part the patient seeks an enacting response, and in part," she continues, "the analyst has an impulse to enact, and some of this will be expressed in the interpretation" (158). One may hear the echo of Tarachow (1962) years earlier: both people, he writes, have "a basic urge to mutual acting out," a human need and wish for a real object (380). Tarachow too locates the analyst's responsibility and function in the act of interpretation: by transforming the real into an *as if*, the analyst opens up possibility and creates the therapeutic realm. And the remarkable psychoanalytic situation thus takes its special shape.

How to maintain sufficient calm while walking on a tightrope? The therapist's work, Pick says, requires a transformation of his or her intense (individual and merely human) conflictual responses—in Freud's language, a working-through. The analyst's capacity to regress and work through the inevitable disturbance allows him (or her) to formulate and give an interpretation: "an integrative creative act" (1985: 158), writes Pick. Crucial here is Pick's idea that, in failing to take our own conflictual responses into account, "we risk enacting that which we should be interpreting" (160)—a step, one might even argue, along a continuum toward exploitation of the transference. Inevitably, according to Pick, the patient will be aware, consciously and unconsciously, of "whether the analyst *evades or meets* the issues" (166, emphasis added).

Meeting rather than evading the issues—a quality of self-aware human presence—is perhaps another way to conceptualize the analyst's mortal gift. Loewald is addressing something similar a year later when he writes:

> For most if not all patients in analysis the analyst's emotional invest-ment, acknowledged or not by either party, is a decisive factor in the curative process ... If a capacity for transference, from its most primi-tive to its most developed form, is a measure of the patient's ana-lyzability, the *capacity for countertransference* is a measure of the analyst's ability to analyze.
>
> (Loewald 1986: 285–286, emphasis added)

Perhaps Pick and Loewald are not so much contradicting as they are elabo-rating Freud's (1915a) "useful warning" to the young doctor "against any tendency to a counter-transference which may be present in his own mind" (160) when the patient falls in love.

Pick (1985) movingly concludes her essay, "[I]f we keep emotions out, we are in danger of keeping out the love which mitigates the hatred, allowing the so-called pursuit of truth to be governed by hatred" (166). Winnicott's 1949 paper "Hate in the Counter-Transference" hovers between the lines. It's hard to imagine a description further from an aso-cial conception of the analytic dyad than this. Two ordinary people sit in Pick's consulting room and both have complex emotional work to do. The analyst, too, has an unconscious. For Pick, however, the differentiation of positions remains absolutely clear. The analyst is responsive but disci-plined, performing the analytic function in the service of the patient. In the commitment to truthfulness, the analyst is alert to his (or her) own internal experience, striving always for balance: the goal, to distinguish between constructive and pathological—or exploitative—uses of the countertrans-ference. Freud is struggling in "Observations on Transference-Love" to capture something similar.

In another image, perhaps more abstract than Pick's tightrope-walking analyst, Jay Greenberg ten years later also accounts for a relationship, exploring what he terms the "interactive matrix": the idea that "every-thing that happens in an analysis reflects the personal contribution of each participant." As Greenberg (1995) puts it, "The concept of an interactive matrix is necessary if we take seriously the idea that there are always two people in the consulting room" (13). It's hard to argue with this statement but, at the same time, it's also easy to read right past it, missing the persistent echo of the young candidate and his peg-analyst, and of Stone's brass monkey. We might pause to wonder that received theory for decades has questioned (a questioning Hoffman claims is ongoing) the fact—is it merely an "idea"?—that there are always two people in the consulting room. Greenberg's sentence, though sensible enough, at the same time dramatizes an absurdity. Anna Freud's comment decades earlier is remarkable in a similar way: "I feel still," she is reported to have said, "that we should leave room somewhere for the realization that analyst and patient are also two real people, of equal adult status, in a real personal relationship to each other" (cited in Greenson and Wexler 1969: 27). At the time that Anna Freud made this statement, such ideas, even stated so tentatively, amounted to apostasy.

Perhaps psychoanalysts are doomed to continue pointing out, at times with absurdly judicious qualification, that there are two people in the consulting room—until a way is found to articulate, sensibly and convincingly, who that second, shadowy figure is. But, closer to the truth, it may be that there *is* no such tidy possibility, the analyst, by definition, a creature shifting shape endlessly, much like the god Proteus, the old man of the sea, whom Menelaus, with his men, lies in wait to subdue and question:

> When he [Proteus] … lay down to sleep … with a shout, we leapt upon him and flung our arms round his back. But the old man's skill and cunning had not deserted him. He began by turning into a bearded lion and then into a snake, and after that a panther and a giant boar. He changed into running water too and a great tree in leaf. But we set our teeth and held him like a vice … "So tell me now" [Menelaus asks], "in your divine omniscience, which god it is that has laid me by the heels and cut my voyage short; and tell me also how I can get home across the playgrounds of the fish."
>
> (Homer, *The Odyssey* 1965: 76)

An analogy might be made here with the patient as Menelaus, the homeward journeying king. Menelaus wrestles with the knowledgeable but slippery old man who holds, Menelaus believes, the answer that would free him from the difficulties that confine him, stalling his journey. Proteus eludes the king, refusing capture by shifting shapes, marvelously—wild animal images, then water and a spectacular tree. How wide-ranging that old wizard's talent, his skill and cunning! The hero king and his men, however, fight like bulldogs: "We set our teeth and held him like a vice."

For a contrasting, less amusing image from the same epic poem, the analyst is sometimes likened to the hero Odysseus tied to the mast, resisting the Sirens. Levine (2010), for example, writes:

> In a well-functioning analytic treatment, the position of the analyst or therapist is akin to that of Odysseus and the Sirens. In order to hear their song, Odysseus knew that he must protect himself from acting on what he heard and felt by having himself restrained. He instructed his crew to plug their ears, leave his ears unplugged, tie him to the mast of the ship and not listen to any of his commands until they had sailed well clear of the Sirens.

Levine then elaborates the metaphor's relevance to the analyst's function:

> It is our professional identity and analytic attitude organized around and reinforced by the presence of the internal third, the ability to maintain an internal analytic frame and perspective about what happens in the treatment, that ties us to the mast of appropriate analytic functioning. This is our necessary rope …
>
> (Levine 2010: 58)

The contrast between this figure of speech—the analyst akin to Odysseus— and Pick's less dramatic tightrope image reflects an important difference of focus. It's not that the Homeric metaphor doesn't effectively capture something about the analyst's position and often turbulent experience, and the self-restraint required. The contrast is a matter of emphasis. The Odyssean metaphor *leads* with the countertransference and elevates the clinician to a central, literally heroic role. This is significantly different from Pick's careful qualification, with the modesty of the less grandiloquent tightrope image—you might call it benignly trite—that emphasizes the analyst's acknowledgment and working-through of his or her own desire and conflictual responses.

In that image of walking a tightrope, the distinction is between two *non*-figurative definitions, that is, between the analyst's "experiencing disturbance" and the analyst's "responding with interpretation that does not convey disturbing anxiety" (Pick 1985: 157). The nature of that disturbance is internal as well as non-specific, and therefore remains open and individual, with neither analyst nor patient cast in any *particular* narrative—range and generosity are implicit. In contrast, the Odysseus metaphor portrays the analyst as the heroic journeyer, with the sirenic patient as seductive, mysterious, and less human: the beautiful and dangerous supernatural sirens lure sailors to their deaths. Somewhat like Sabina Spielrein, the patient is cast as a natural force (see Chapter 3). Or, perhaps more troubling, as a supernatural creature (is she a witch?), full of trickery, and impossible to resist. Levine's analyst-as-Odysseus relies on restraints such as "professional identity and analytic attitude" conceptualized as ropes (reinforced by "the internal third," etc.) tying him "to the mast of appropriate analytic functioning."

In yet another striking image, Renik presents an analyst who is also a figurative adventurer of sorts, but one imagined in motion, and freer from restraints. Renik (1993a) poses an essential question: "how are we to say where analytic work leaves off and exploitation of the analytic situation begins?" (565). For Renik, as for Levine, the concern is the analyst's ethical practice in the presence of strain, uncertainty, and temptation. To that purpose, Renik (1993a) suggests a shift in metaphors to best protect the dyad:

> Instead of the analyst as surgeon or reflecting mirror our guiding metaphor might be the analyst as skier or surfer—someone who allows himself or herself to be acted upon by powerful forces, knowing that they are to be managed and harnessed, rather than completely controlled.

Here he pauses to qualify what he's said, perhaps confronting an anxiety:

> Of course, the forces with which an analyst contends in his or her work are internal ones. In this sense, perhaps we should think of effective clinical psychoanalytic practice as not unlike good sex, in that it is impossible to arrive at the desired outcome without, in some measure, relinquishing self-control as a goal.
>
> (Renik 1993a: 565)

The analyst imagined here is having a thrilling experience, again leading with the countertransference: he is the focus of attention—performing, an athlete riding the waves and "acted upon by powerful forces" until the culminating "desired outcome." Like the seafarer Odysseus, the surfer or the skier heroically sustains driving forces (the tides, the elements, the mountain slopes) that he must "manage" and "harness."

What in the simile ("not un*like*") restrains this analyst? First disclaiming the suggestiveness of the images ("Of course, the forces with which the analyst contends ... are internal ones"), Renik extends the analogy, introducing the simile with its double negative to conceptualize the analyst's effective practice—the equivocal wording a further disclaimer regarding "good sex." One thinks of Freud's (1915a) warning to the young doctor in "Observations on Transference-Love": it is not always easy "to keep within the limits prescribed by ethics and technique," in particular for those "still youngish"; a woman's natural appeal, especially a woman "of high principles who confesses her passion," brings with it "the danger of making a man forget his technique and his medical task for the sake of a fine experience" (169–170). The sirens, and the cresting waves, are not individuals with volition but more akin to mere circumstances. Renik's narrative focus here is on the epic hero—that is, the analyst—pursuing his journey, or the athlete accomplishing his feat. One could say something similar about Freud's young doctor eighty years earlier, and his experience of the appealing woman who "sues for love" (170): the analyst's struggle to resist her (she is *thrilling*) is the focus.

In the privacy of the consulting room, who *is* the analyst conceived as "a skier or surfer," in a process "not unlike good sex"? On the one hand, Renik's passage is in itself innocent—the surfer is not the analyst having sex with the patient—and his crucial point is that awareness and acknowledgment of temptation protects both people better than denial. But on the other hand, the intentionally provocative language, in psychoanalysis of all fields, must have layers of meaning. Analytic work unfolds, Renik (1993b) also writes, "via a process of continuous, mutually active embroilment between analyst and analysand" (138). To be "embroiled" is to be dragged in, swept up, with connotations of force and danger—a messier situation than simply being "involved."

What can language like "mutually active embroilment" and "not unlike good sex" tell us about persistent questions: What is an analyst, and what is the therapeutic offering? What are the benefits, what the risks? To lose a wooden peg, or a brass monkey, is quite different—perhaps a polar opposite—from the loss of the charismatic flesh-and-blood embroiled hero. What do these opposites mean, separately and as a polarity, and what image or metaphor (if there is any) between the extremes might be better? Historically, the analyst has been conceived and reconceived, to the point of comedy, to name only a few: from mirror to screen to surgeon to sculptor to parental figure to director to witness to container to midwife to music teacher to mutual self-inquirer to skilled assistant to field manager to wizard to athlete to cook to fellow explorer to co-actor to co-creator to Homeric hero to artist or poet.

...

Defining the nature of the analyst and the analytic function has entailed multiple figures and an elaborate jargon, often conveying increased temperature and turmoil. Why is that so? What, exactly, is the discomfort in the analyst's position? What (at worst) is being covered over or avoided—or (at best) revealed? I'd like to look a bit more closely at three examples, arranged on a continuum, that I find useful to give the analyst form, and to track shifts over time in how the analyst is conceptualized: the analyst conceived as a telephone receiver (Freud, 1912b); as a parental figure safe-keeping a vision (Loewald, 1960); and, last, as a skilled assistant (Poland, 1996 [1984]). With that historical progression—parallel to what has been referred to, somewhat schematically, as the shift from a "one-person" to a "two-person" psychology—the analyst becomes less detached, more affectively involved, the endeavor more collaborative. In each of these instances, what would it mean to lose such a therapist? The metaphors have different implications for the loss, as well as for the analyst's job and for understanding the risks.

Freud, who understood early the explosive potential of the psycho-analytic situation, offered the young doctor guides and first principles. Conceived as cool, aloof, and relatively uninvolved with the patient, the analyst verges, in a caricature, on being inanimate: a blank screen, or a reflecting mirror. Striving for detachment, for neutrality, he proceeds according to rules of technique—Freud's own term, it's important to keep in mind, is "recommendations," not "rules," a flexibility implicit—applied with little variation across the range of suitable patients. The clinician's personality, in that conception, is relatively inconsequential; what matters is a capacity to use what Otto Isakower later called the "analyzing instrument" (1963), the counterpart to the patient's free associations.

In imagining such an "instrument," one may think first of the surgeon's scalpel rather than the telephone. Isakower's instrument, however, is a humane metaphor elaborating the quality of the analyst's attentiveness—similar to Freud's (1912c) description of the doctor's "evenly-suspended attention" (111–112). As McLaughlin (1981) puts it, the analyzing instrument refers to "the conjoined operation of two minds, patient's and analyst's, working together in a goal-specific intent" (658; see also Balter, Lothane, and Spencer, 1980; Grossman, 1992). The term "instrument," of course, can include not only the scalpel and the telephone, but the microscope, the thermometer, and the violin. To be *instrumental* is to be part of a process, the furthest thing from inanimate or static.

In any case, the psychoanalytic situation in that early model is conceived not chiefly as an interaction—an austerity often exaggerated by later generations. The analytic instrument guides the clinician to formulate interpretations, and interpretation can lead to insight, a route toward cure. Over the years many inanimate similes have been generated. Each emphasizes the therapist's role as one who apprehends the truth, linking the activity to the functions of a non-human object or mechanism. Freud writes:

> [The analyst] must turn his own unconscious like a receptive organ towards the transmitting unconscious of the patient. He must adjust himself to the patient as a telephone receiver is adjusted to the transmitting microphone. Just as the receiver converts into sound-waves the electric oscillations in the telephone line which were set up by sound-waves, so the doctor's unconscious is able, from the derivatives of the unconscious which are communicated to him, to reconstruct that unconscious, which has determined the patient's free associations.
>
> (Freud 1912b: 115–116)

The idea of the therapist as a decoder who ferrets out (or translates) the patient's unconscious message has endured. Rangell writes:

> I visualize the beginning stages of an analytic relationship as a relay race, in which a runner hands the baton to a partner, who then runs with it on his behalf. There is one important difference: that in this case the baton, that is, the key to the first runner's mind, is handed to the other, the analyst, for both to run along together. The analyst, or analytic therapist, accompanies the analysand on his journey

during the course of the treatment process ... At the termination of the therapeutic experience, the accompanying life traveler relinquishes his grip on the baton, which the patient continues to hold alone ...

(Rangell 1996: 144)

Here Rangell mixes old and new, animate (runner) and inanimate (baton). As with Freud's telephone and Isakower's instrument, patient and therapist work together: They are partners, undertaking a journey. In Rangell's image, the runner-patient hands the baton to the accompanying traveler but, unlike in a relay race, the two runners continue on together—in a sense, they become one, the first racer passing the key to his mind over to the second. Like the baton, the key is a technical and metallic image, suggesting that one person unlocks and views what is inside the other, as if solving a puzzle. Although the two run together, the image conveys little explicit sense of emotional involvement, consistent with the conception of the analyst as distant and detached. The therapist is impersonal, expert, and accurate—in Hoffman's term, asocial.

In Hans Loewald's paper "On the Therapeutic Action of Psychoanalysis," the venture becomes more personal. Influenced by earlier thinkers like Mahler, Spitz, and Winnicott, Loewald (1960) introduces a new metaphor, describing the interactions between analyst and patient as "comparable in their structure and significance to the early understanding between mother and child" (239). The so-called classical position understands the mind as a closed system, the analyst not a co-actor but "a reflecting mirror," he writes, "albeit of the unconscious, and characterized by scrupulous neutrality" (223). Loewald amends that position:

There is a tendency to consider the analyst's availability as an object merely as a device ... seen in terms of his being a screen or mirror onto which the patient projects his transferences, and which reflect them back to him in the form of interpretations. In this view, at the ideal termination point of analysis no further transference occurs, no projections are thrown on the mirror; the mirror, having nothing new to reflect, can be discarded. This is only a half-truth.

(Loewald 1960: 225)

The analyst no longer serves merely as a device for objectively interpreting the patient's reality, nor is the therapeutic interaction limited to that provision. In seeking out the nature of the rest of the provision—the analyst as new object, the other half of the truth making it "whole"—Loewald (1960) distinguishes the objectivity of the analyst from the objectivity of a scientist: the former, he tells us, "should not be confused with the 'neutral' attitude of the pure scientist toward the subject of his study" (226).

In Loewald's (1960) writing a new kind of animating language emerges: the analyst's attitude involves "love and respect for the individual and for individual development" (229). Elsewhere he writes, in a similar vein: "in our best moments of dispassionate and objective analyzing we love our object, the patient, more than at any other time and are compassionate with his whole being" (1980 [1970]: 297)—a pairing of detachment and commitment that expresses analytic attitude and purpose as well as discipline. Loewald offers the new figure, likening its workings to a parental function:

> The parent ideally is in an empathic relationship of understanding the child's particular stage in development, yet ahead in his vision of the child's future and mediating this vision to the child in his dealing with him. This vision, informed by the parent's own experience and knowledge of growth and future, is, ideally, a more articulate and more integrated version of the core of being that the child presents to the parent. This "more" that the parent sees and knows, he mediates to the child so that the child in identification with it can grow.
>
> (Loewald 1980 [1960]: 229)

He describes how that "more" is mediated:

> The child, by internalizing aspects of the parent, also internalizes the parent's image of the child—an image that is mediated to the child in the thousand different ways of being handled, bodily and emotionally … The child begins to experience himself as a centered unit by being centered upon.
>
> (Loewald 1980 [1960]: 230)

This quasi-parental "more" that the analyst perceives—an image of the person's potential—is mediated and reflected back to the patient so that he may integrate it and, by identification with it, grow. The analyst safe-keeps that "vision."

To capture the idea of a keep-safe, Loewald invokes the figure of a sculptor, taking the metaphor from Freud, who borrows it from Leonardo da Vinci:

> ... as Freud has beautifully put it, using an expression of Leonardo da Vinci, *pervia di levare* as in sculpturing, not *pervia di porre* as in painting. In sculpturing, the figure to be created comes into being by taking something away from the material; in painting by adding something to the canvas. In analysis, we bring about the true form by taking away the neurotic distortions. However, as in sculpture, we must have, if only in rudiments, an image of that which needs to be brought into its own. The patient, by revealing himself to the analyst, provides rudiments of such an image through all the distortions—an image that the analyst has to focus in his mind, thus *holding it in safe-keeping* for the patient to whom it is mainly lost.
>
> (Loewald 1980 [1960]: 225–226, emphasis added)

The analyst, somewhat like the sculptor, removes something (neurotic distortions, obstructions to growth) so that a shape emerges; but he does not, as in painting, *add* material to create the image. Safe-keeping is functional—a removal to reveal—and involves disciplined principles of care—restraint, non-imposition—related to the ideals of abstinence and neutrality. This safe-keeping is not a molding in the analyst's image; rather, the analyst's activity, including interpretation, is non-intrusive, non-controlling. Tact is involved: how much to direct, how much to hold back.

In ways like these, Loewald reconceives and enlarges the analyst. No longer merely a mechanistic device, nor a purely objective purveyor of insight, Loewald's analyst is humanized and his particularity legitimized: he is a respectful, responsive keeper of value. Loewald re-*pictures* the analyst, but the form that the analyst's humanness takes is not prescribed. Loewald's precision is reminiscent of Pick, whose tightrope walking analyst's human responsiveness is both individual and particular to the dyad. (No pegs or brass toys here: my analyst is *my* analyst, yours is yours.) The patient's freedom and future are safe-kept in this humane, disciplined attitude.

More proactive than Loewald's safe-keeping is Warren Poland's metaphor of the skilled assistant. Echoing Loewald, Poland (1996 [1984]) writes that the analyst "functions not simply on the basis of who the

observed patient *is*, but also on the sense of what the patient *might become*"
(99, emphasis in original). However, Poland's idea pointedly qualifies the
authority of "knower." Whereas Loewald's analyst, somewhat like a parent, is "ahead in his vision," and to some extent an objectively knowing
observer, for Poland, one can know one's own mind but can only know
about another's. Loewald's (1975) analyst, like Poland's, participates in
the treatment artifice—conspiring with the patient "in the creation of an
illusion, a play"—but unlike Poland's analyst, he is cast as director of the
play-like situation (279–280).

Poland (1996 [1984]) introduces the new figure: "The analyst is a technically skilled assistant at work in the patient's service, welcomed into
this other person's life to serve a very special function" (100). That function? The patient has a collaborator, a companion in the exploration of the
patient's mind. The "assistant"—a term positioning the therapist humbly
in relation to patient-as-foreman—offers his best understanding rather
than absolute knowledge: "Uncompromising efforts toward insight are the
most an analyst can give a patient, a gift unique and more valuable than
any transference gratification" (90). The well-spring of the analytic gift,
one might say, is in the integrity of striving: Poland's "uncompromising
efforts toward insight."

Poland (1996 [1984]) carefully distinguishes between "insight" and
"understanding," the former involving self-knowledge, the latter knowledge and appreciation of another's mind. Analytic insight is achieved in
the context of the relationship, but one cannot know an "other" the same
way that one knows oneself: "An analyst cannot *give* an insight" because
insight is knowledge—*self*-knowledge (65). Instead the therapist's understanding helps the patient arrive at insight; through this focused collaboration the patient can come to know himself or herself.

"To understand the other," Poland (1996 [1984]) writes, "is to plunge
along with the other" (70). In striking contrast to the cool revelatory role
of the earlier model, this analyst "plunges along" with the patient—two
people in a headlong immersion, the verb connoting impetuous if not
quite reckless downward motion. Over time, Poland's skilled assistant
comes to appreciate the workings of the patient's mind, always respect-
ing the patient as the one who knows best. The plunging-along analyst
might be conceived of as on a continuum somewhere between Rangell's
detached baton-wielding runner-companion and Renik's embroiled surfer.
Poland significantly writes "plunges along" instead of "plunges in"—his

skilled assistant is a proactive figure, but judiciously characterized as more *instrumental* than embroiled.

To recapitulate: in the intricate weaving that is twentieth-century psychoanalytic thought, the analyst's affective presence has been a central thread. The patient's intensity of engagement has been assumed since the beginning. Over time, the analyst's emotional involvement, always implicit, becomes more straightforwardly acknowledged. Sometimes it is even the focus. Within one current of the professional literature, the language has become increasingly—at times even giddily—suggestive, with phrases such as "the intimate edge," "love in the afternoon," "the hug and the hard-on," and "not unlike good sex."[3]

How to find the line between acceptable and exploitative, between involvement and embroilment, between instrument and intrusion? Such questions recall the heat involved in Breuer's supposed flight from Anna O and the sexual transgressions among some of Freud's early followers. In his efforts to understand his own invention, Freud's technical cautions were geared to rescue the psychoanalytic situation: he understood that both participants, merely mortals, needed protection if they were to use the extraordinary arrangement to accomplish the work for which it was intended.

At the outset, then, the issues already include how to assess the danger while offering that protection. Freud addresses these risks and pitfalls in *Papers on Technique*. The situation is inherently prone to heating up: the analyst, in one of Freud's early metaphors, serving as a "catalytic ferment," stirring things up but not himself affected. Today's analytic thinking acknowledges openly that the intensity and stimulation are not only inevitable but reciprocal. What remains less clear today, however, is where the analyst locates the guides necessary for managing the *explosive forces* (Freud) in an *embroilment not unlike good sex* (Renik) into which he or she *plunges* (Poland).

Like anxiety, suggestive language too has been present from the start. In "Observations on Transference-Love" Freud confronts the analyst's temptation to ethical misconduct—treatment fails: a "coming to grief." In this first discussion of indispensable terms, Freud establishes—let me emphasize once again—that the ethical and the technical are inseparable. Struggling here at the inception to find adequate language for the erotic forces stirred in treatment, Freud also anticipates the most important ongoing questions: How will the analyst comprehend the transference intensity, how manage it, how respond? There are "unruly forces" released in the analyst as well: the analyst's countertransference is the true, though partly submerged, topic of this essay.

Freud (1915a) asks: "But how is the analyst to behave in order not to come to grief over this situation, supposing he is convinced that the treatment should be carried on in spite of this erotic transference?" (163). In other words, he is exploring the temptation for the analyst to exploit the transference. Freud is often criticized for holding an unrealistic view of countertransference as something the analyst must rise above. But "Observations on Transference-Love" records his own lucid, deep, real-time uneasiness: a struggle to accept the reality of the analyst's human vulnerability (we could say "mortal" vulnerability) in the combustion.

I'll return to something I've earlier identified as a queasy, uncomfortable, maybe even alienating moment in this fundamental paper (see Chapter 2). Close to the end, in summing up the argument for the doctor to restrain himself "from giving the patient his love," Freud allows himself to make an off-color joke—a smutty chuckle imbedded in the peroration. Here is Strachey's translation:

> [The doctor] must not stage the scene of a dog-race in which the prize was to be a garland of sausages but which some humorist spoilt by throwing a single sausage on to the track. The result was, of course, that the dogs threw themselves upon it and forgot all about the race and about the garland that was luring them to victory in the far distance.
>
> (Freud 1915a: 169)

Leading up to the joke, Freud (1915a) has restated, unequivocally, in plain language, the doctor's responsibility: "[the analyst] must not derive any personal advantage from [the transference love]. The patient's willingness makes no difference; it merely throws the whole responsibility on the analyst himself" (169). The ethical combines with the technical to restrain him from giving her his love: if she is to have access to her capacity for love, she mustn't fritter it away in treatment but instead save it for real life. The sausage gag follows.

Freud deftly mixes the high with the low—the ethical sits alongside the smutty chuckle. I smirk too. Yet my smirk is a bit uncomfortable. Certainly there's nothing unusual in this kind of play. It's an ancient tradition. Here is the Italian poet Boccaccio in the fourteenth century: "Men and women generally … go around all day long saying 'hole' and 'rod' and 'mortar' and 'pestle' and 'sausage' and 'mortadella' and lots of other things like that" (from *The Decameron*). A sausage was never just a sausage, even in the fourteenth century; and who better than a psychoanalyst to appreciate how, with a joke, one bypasses the censors, deriving pleasure from dangerous feelings—hostility, aggression, excitement. In his treatise on jokes Freud asks why people joke *together*, speaking to a social process: jokes say something about social life. The psychoanalytic literature, too, is a social process.

Is it the community of doctors Freud laughs with, willing to demean the situation in order to reassure that community and himself? Who's the avid one in the joke, who's the dog, who's the "humorist"?—In German, the word is *spassvogel*, or "funny bird"; the spoiler is a *spassvogel*, which Joan Riviere translates as "funny fellow," a prankster who messes up the orderly race. To my ear, that word lightens the joke a bit, although it doesn't erase the queasy feeling. I detect a note of nervous performance and excited unease—call it an overstimulated quality that manifests the very thing he's trying to control. Perhaps Freud deals with this discombobulation by becoming a bit of a provocative *spassvogel* himself.

As to another bit of language, there is Freud's phrase that the analyst might "come to grief" (in German, *zu scheitern*, meaning something closer to "fail" or "break down"). The English idiom, bringing in "grief," aptly captures the doctor's regretful failure to protect the treatment, but the passage, in either language, fails even to mention the vulnerability and pain—and possibly grief—of the patient, who here is objectified, while the doctor is humanized. I'm reminded (again) of how Jung and Freud, in their correspondence, talk about Sabina Spielrein. Jung asserts, "She was of course systematically planning my seduction"; and Freud consoles Jung: "No lasting harm is done … [These experiences] help us to develop the thick skin we need and to dominate 'counter-transference' … they are a blessing in disguise" (McGuire 1974: 229–231). This correspondence comes five years before "Observations on Transference-Love" with its warned-against "fine experience." Here too, in this exchange, the woman patient who falls in love with the doctor is treated as an impersonal and threatening force of nature. The patient's situation, we all know, may entail, beyond grief, lasting harm.

Finally, there's the doctor's grief, also covered-over by the joke: the analyst's own unanalyzed sadness, perhaps including Freud's own, avoided or deflected. The intrusion of the *spassvogel*, the dog race, the single sausage distracting from the garland of sausages is itself a kind of narrative or compositional prank, a displacement by Freud, the writer. He directs us to the doctor's "coming to grief," by which he means, because of the situation (*dieser Situation*) the treatment fails for the analyst. But he also distracts from another kind of loss for the patient. There is no tenderness in the joke, which deflects grief and anxiety with comedy. It's not just the grief for the patient that's skirted, but the grief of, and grief *for*, the doctor: lamenting whatever flaw or problem has led him to misuse the patient this way. Perhaps there's also Freud's foreboding that his entire project, already endangered—as he is discovering—may in time "come to grief" as well.

The dogs are not simply the woman, any more than the sausage is simply a penis. The animals avid for the sausage are the many-headed analytic process itself, and the forces it stirs. To put it another way, doctor and patient together are the dogs, both present, as are the phallic sausage and the yonic garland. And the *spassvogel*/funny fellow is life itself, human nature, in all its fallibility and vulnerability.

And in relation to our human nature: how do we think about the patient's grief when the analyst dies? By examining these similes and metaphors for the analyst and the analytic process, I have hoped to illuminate not only the nature of the loss but the nature of the psychoanalytic situation as well. These examples of figurative language may also shed light on the century-long, nearly total neglect of the analyst's mortality. Analysts have an unusual kind of power in their professional role. Treatment *works* by the analyst becoming important to people, in whatever individual ways they will make that figure important: the analyst aims to matter. The psychoanalytic situation, as I have emphasized throughout, is a professional encounter purposefully configured to intensify that mattering. But if the aim is to *matter*, and the analyst sets out to court that condition—Freud's "catalytic ferment"—what is it for that human catalyst to die? The work proceeds by structured limitation, the eventual ending intimated from the very first hour. But that finality is not supposed to happen through the analyst's death.

Insofar as one moves toward conceiving the analyst in terms of devices or machines, one moves away from conceiving that person as human— and, mortal. An inanimate mechanism doesn't matter, the young psychoanalytic candidate notes, except as a hook for attitudes. The old view of the therapeutic relationship considered countertransference a problem. The analyst in that view is instructed to erase himself: the patient's subjectivity is at the center, the analyst serving as a means to reflect its form. At an extreme, which in an earlier chapter I've called the Olympian delusion, the analyst is conceptualized as *above* being a subject himself, a notion that brings with it the danger of dissolving the line that keeps the patient safe. Where there is only one entity, the therapist believing in an heroic capacity for selflessness, there can be no separation.

For later thinking, in contrast, the analyst's countertransference is not only acceptable but considered essential to the process. Working through one's affective presence has moved toward the center of the analyst's job. However, alertness to countertransference while also keeping one's balance (Irma Brenman Pick's tightrope walker) is quite different from *privileging* the analyst's experience: a shift in emphasis tending, in the worst case, to dehumanize the patient. In the early years, the psychoanalyst might be conceived as cool, unaffected, superior, and uninvolved—entitled to abnegate ordinary human kindness and consideration. But easy gestures of humility (things like, "the analyst is no longer authoritarian"; or, "the clinical interaction is a collaboration of peers") can also mask an abnegation of responsibility, inviting that same danger of obscuring the line that keeps the patient safe.

To lose a safe-keeper/guide is different from losing a wooden peg, at one end of a continuum. Neither, at the other end, is that loss the same as losing the charismatic hero/performer. But perhaps the hero-analyst (or the performer-analyst) can be already lost: in a reversal, by becoming the protagonist, his subjectivity—or, less politely, his narcissism—may have in effect diminished or effaced the central drama of the patient. At such an extreme, again, the dyad is reduced to a single subjectivity: the obverse of the Olympian delusion—equally preening, perhaps equally prone to exploiting the patient.

Winnicott, like Pick, captures the intensity of the analyst's inevitable struggle to keep his balance. As to the clinician's most central task:

> The essential feature is the analyst's survival and the intactness of the psychoanalytic technique. Imagine how traumatic can be the actual death of the analyst when this kind of work is in process, although even the actual death of the analyst is not as bad as the development in the analyst of a change toward retaliation.
>
> (Winnicott 1969: 714)

The virtual death, to reiterate, may be more destructive, and more absolute, than the actual death. The quasi-Jovian elevation—as to an immortal bull or swan or eagle—betrays the process (see Chapter 2). Human imperfection animates the work: the psychoanalyst at any moment can err and can also die. "These are risks," Winnicott adds, "that simply must be taken by the patient." The analyst who survives, in Winnicott's sense, has held the seat.

...

And what, when the therapist dies, has the patient *not* lost? What is the redeeming virtue of such a crazy business? The Chilean poet Pablo Neruda, in a brief essay called "Childhood and Poetry" (1993), tells a story about an early memory. One day, playing alone in a backyard lot, he finds a hole in a fence board; looking through the hole he sees a wild, uncared for landscape just like the lonely one he stands in. He steps back:

> All of a sudden a hand appeared, a tiny hand of a boy about my own age. By the time I came close again, the hand was gone, and in its place there was a marvelous white sheep.
>
> The sheep's wool was faded. Its wheels had escaped. All of this only made it more authentic. I had never seen such a wonderful sheep. I looked back through the hole but the boy had disappeared. I went into the house and brought out a treasure of my own: a pinecone, opened, full of odor and resin, which I adored. I set it down in the same spot and went off with the sheep.
>
> I never saw either the hand or the boy again. And I have never again seen a sheep like that either. The toy I lost finally in a fire. But even now ... whenever I pass a toy shop, I look furtively into the window, but it's no use. They don't make sheep like that any more.

Neruda ends the story:

> Maybe it was nothing but a game two boys played who didn't know each other and wanted to pass to the other some good things of life. Yet maybe this small and mysterious exchange of gifts remained inside me, deep and indestructible, giving my poetry light.
>
> (Neruda 1993: 12–13)

In this little allegory the two small boys don't see each other and they never meet again. But, the story tells us, there is no gift outside of relationship; and the power, much like the power of the psychoanalytic situation, is in its formal limitation—deep and indestructible, the exchange remains inside of the boy, giving his poetry light.

Imperfection and mortality are part of the psychoanalytic form. The process proceeds, one could say, with the analyst's managing, well enough, the anxiety of mutability: mortal anxiety, along with erotic anxiety, is integral to the success of treatment. Without mortality—human vulnerability—there are no ghosts, and without ghosts there are no ancestors. Unless the analyst too, like the patient, meets the built-in risk, and confronts the danger, there is also no gift.

That redemption is exemplified in Loewald's beautiful passage on ghosts and ancestors:

> The transference neurosis, in the technical sense of the establishment and resolution of it in the analytic process, is due to the blood of recognition, which the patient's unconscious is given to taste so that the old ghosts may reawaken to life. Those who know ghosts tell us that they long to be released from their ghost life and led to rest as ancestors. As ancestors they live forth in the present generation, while as ghosts they are compelled to haunt the present generation with their shadow life. Transference is pathological insofar as the unconscious is a crowd of ghosts, and this is the beginning of the transference neurosis in analysis: ghosts of the unconscious, imprisoned by defenses but haunting the patient in the dark of his defenses and symptoms, are allowed to taste blood, are let loose. In the daylight of analysis the ghosts of the unconscious are laid and led to rest as ancestors ...
>
> (Loewald 1980 [1960]: 248–249)

I had read this well-known passage many times without noticing the remarkable wording: "laid and led to rest as ancestors"—the compressed verb phrase an example of Loewald's "magical-evocative" function of language, the power of words (1980 [1970]: 199). What does Loewald accomplish here with the seeming illogic of these five words, "laid and led to rest"? How can ghosts be *led* to rest after they've already been *laid* to rest? It must be the nature of ghosts!

The two verbs—"lay" and "lead"—are entirely different although, lulled by sounds, "laid and led," we may hardly notice. The actual logic, however, is exquisite: the general sense of the verb "lay," for example, is to cause to lie (down). Ghosts can be led to rest in no other way than first to be laid to rest. In an archaic sense of the word, "to lay (a spirit)" is to prevent a spirit from walking. The analytic task we call working through perhaps resembles a "laying to rest," at which point only, if sufficiently accomplished, can the ghost be *led* to rest as ancestor. "To lay to rest" is to bury a body—in that sense a funeral rite of safe-keeping, and a practical action of care and respect.

In ways like these, Loewald's evocative language reflects his own safe-keeping. The idea of "keep-safe"—whether that is the analyst's safe-keeping the patient's future, or Loewald's safe-keeping psychoanalysis itself—is embedded in the ghosts to ancestors passage: something of value protected, preserved, and transmitted across centuries and generations, from Homer to Freud, through Loewald who passes it on, having also made it his own, to the psychoanalytic generations that come after. Loewald consistently finds a tone that balances authority and humanity: safe-keeper is not, in the end, merely an office of authority but, rather, *more*: a position of reliability. The moral and intellectual tact is reflected in the prose. In his rhetoric, Loewald alternates philosophy and psychoanalysis, the abstract conceptualizing, and the practice of care-taking. He goes from the one to the other, enacting that dialectic, over and over.

Loewald intermixes different levels of thought and language which, in the process, refresh each other and heighten the work: a reciprocal enlivening not only between people, enabling them to grow, but within persons—the mind cycling up, in Friedman's (2008b) words, "into a world where it finds more definition, and takes that definition down to old, primal urges, which then shoot up again, transformed, like a hermeneutic garden fountain" (1107).

Taking a leaf from Loewald's book, I'll end with Freud on psychoanalysis, the analytic task, and spirits:

> To urge the patient to suppress, renounce, or sublimate her instincts the moment she has admitted her erotic transference would be, not an analytic way of dealing with them, but a senseless one. It would be just as though, after summoning up a spirit from the underworld by cunning spells, one were to send him down again without having asked him a single question.

> (Freud 1915a: 164)

Notes

1 Portions of this chapter have appeared, in slightly different form, as part of "Loewald Panel: Discussion," in *Journal of the American Psychoanalytic Association*, 56 (2008): 1129–1137.

2 It's not my purpose here to review the extensive countertransference literature. I let Pick's paper represent the burgeoning interest in the analyst's countertransference in the last forty or fifty years. For a good review of the countertransference literature before 1980, see McLaughlin (1981).

3 See Ehrenberg, *The Intimate Edge* (1992); Davies, "Love in the Afternoon" (1994); "The Hug and the Hard-On" comes from Dimen, "*Lapsus Linguae* or, A Slip of the Tongue?" (2011); "not unlike good sex" comes from Renik (1993a).

Epilogue[1]

I have been a lucky man. To feel the intimacy of brothers is a marvelous thing in life. To feel the love of people whom we love is a fire that feeds our life. But to feel the affection that comes from those whom we do not know, from those unknown to us, who are watching over our sleep and solitude, over our dangers and our weaknesses—that is something still greater and more beautiful because it widens out the boundaries of our being, and unites all living things.

— Pablo Neruda, "Childhood and Poetry"

When my therapist, Joseph Nemetz, suddenly died, I had been working with him in an intensive psychotherapy, two and three times a week, for more than four years. Nemetz's professional conduct, in retrospect, serves as an implicit critique of the inadequate professional literature regarding the central matter of the therapist's mortality in both primary senses.

I had asked several weeks earlier if we could talk about my beginning analysis. Nemetz was surprised by my request, and I by his surprise. I thought I had made many less-than-subtle hints about analysis. I told him I thought I had been reasonably clear; he replied that he had not understood me. Possibly, both of us were right. I came to wonder later whether I had in fact been quite clear but that his usual capacity to hear me had in this particular matter broken down: did he wish *not* to hear me? I've wondered whether his deafness to my hints came from his intuitive understanding that, if I were to ask, he would have to say no—the answer he'd be compelled, as I now understand, to give. With the refusal, I would, if I wanted analysis enough, move to another therapist. I believe that he cared very much about me, enjoyed his work with me, and preferred that I not leave him.

He didn't answer me right away. He told me that, because of his age (he was seventy-one), he was cautious about beginning new analyses; when I asked if our four years of work together made no difference, he answered that of course it did, and that he would need some time to think about it. Over the next ten days I argued my case, growing more excited and hopeful as the days passed and he did not refuse.

Several minutes into our fifth meeting after I had first asked to begin analysis, I was speaking with an animation every minute moving closer to pleased assumption: I *would* have my wish. I remember that he lifted his hand lightly, several inches off his knee, in a gesture that stopped me dead—a "Whoa!" to a racing horse. The very long silence lasted perhaps five seconds, and then he spoke quietly:

"There's more than one person in this room to be considered," he said.

I was speechless. At that moment and in that pause, I caught a clear glimpse of him, perhaps for the first time in ten days, so hard had I been working to obliterate him in order to have what I wanted. I saw something then about what he might feel, what he might wish, and what this decision might mean for him. I was able then to say, calmly and with tremendous sadness, "This must be hard for you too." He nodded very slightly and said, "In many ways."

Although he didn't give me his answer until the next time we met, I knew then what he would likely say and began to prepare myself for it. Sometimes I think I'd really known the answer from the beginning, maybe even before he did, and my wish not to hear what I already knew explained my impetuous rush to fill with words any space for an honest exchange with him. My unconscious hope was to keep both of us from deeper reflection; but he didn't give up that responsibility.

Near the start of our next meeting, he said that, given the nature of my own losses, and the power of analysis, and given the good possibility that he might die before the work was done, analysis with him was not a good idea; he said that, if I wanted analysis, he'd help me arrange it. I knew that, given his love for the work, and especially for that work from behind the couch, his decision was not easy. But I also knew in a hazy way that it was his commitment to the work, and to me, that guided his decision.

I asked him if he'd ever changed his mind about anything, and he replied, quickly and very gently, "I once decided not to be a cowboy." As was often true in my time with this man, my laughter was part of the power of the moment: few people have ever looked *less* like a cowboy. My tears and rage followed.

But I didn't fully understand his words for a long time. Many months after his death, I did understand that Dr. Nemetz was telling me far more than, "No, I can't be your analyst." He was telling me that, however much he might wish to give me what I wanted, he couldn't change his mind because any other decision, *by his lights*, would be wild and incautious. His refusal was dictated by his understanding of and respect for the power of the analytic process, for his own human limitations, and for me. With that decision I think he looked squarely at the ending of his life work, and of his life. At some point I also understood his remark—"I once decided not to be a cowboy"—I understood it as a rejection of the charismatic style of certain analysts. I use the word "charismatic" here in the pejorative sense. Nemetz had the capacity to bear the responsibility of "No," and at the moment he spoke, it was to remind me that there are *always* two individual, mortal people in the consulting room. And in that quiet reminder is located the most essential principle guarding the patient's safety.

A few weeks later, on a Wednesday in mid-May, the hour came to a close. I remained angry at him. He was going away for the weekend to a conference in Philadelphia. He often ended an hour with something intended to leave me thinking. This time it was a question. His last words to me were: "What have I done to make you think I don't understand how disappointed you are?"

I paused and said, "I'll think about it, and I'll let you know Monday morning." I stood up and left him with my usual tag line when he went away to meetings: "Have a good time, learn something, and cross the street very carefully." He collapsed without warning on Sunday in the airport in Philadelphia, and he died six days later, apparently never regaining consciousness.

Note

1 This text originally appeared, in a slightly different form, as part of "A Symposium on the Dead," in *The Threepenny Review*, 96 (Winter 2004): 28–29. Reprinted with permission.

References

Almond, Richard (2011). "Freud's 'The Dynamics of Transference' One Hundred Years Later." *Journal of the American Psychoanalytic Association*, 59: 1129–1156

Aurelius, Marcus (2010). *Meditations, Book 2*. Trans. George Long. Guilford, CT: White Crow Books.

Balter, Leon, Lothane, Zvi, & Spencer, James (1980). "On the Analyzing Instrument." *Psychoanalytic Quarterly*, 49: 474–504.

Bergmann, Martin (1986). "Transference Love and Love in Real Life." *International Journal of Psychoanalytic Psychotherapy*, 11: 27–45.

— (1997). "Termination: The Achilles Heel of Psychoanalytic Technique." *Psychoanalytic Psychotherapy*, 14: 163–174.

— (2004). *Understanding Dissidence and Controversy in the History of Psychoanalysis*. New York, NY: Other Press.

Bird, Brian (1972). "Notes on Transference: Universal Phenomenon and Hardest Part of Analysis." *Journal of the American Psychoanalytic Association*, 20: 267–301.

Blum, Harold (1981). "The Forbidden Quest and the Analytic Ideal: The Superego and Insight." *Psychoanalytic Quarterly*, 50: 535–556.

— (1989). "The Concept of Termination and the Evolution of Psychoanalytic Thought." *Journal of the American Psychoanalytic Association*, 37: 275–295.

Boccaccio, Giovanni (2016). *The Decameron*. Trans. and ed. Wayne Rebhorn. New York, NY: W. W. Norton & Co.

Breuer, Josef & Freud, Sigmund (1895). *Studies on Hysteria. S. E., 2*. London: Hogarth Press.

Bulfinch, Thomas (1964). *Bulfinch's Mythology*. London: Spring Books.

Calef, Victor & Weinshel, Edward (1980). "The Analyst as Conscience of the Analysis." *International Review of Psychoanalysis*, 8: 279–290.

Carotenuto, Aldo (1982). *A Secret Symmetry: Sabina Spielrein between Jung and Freud*. Trans. Arno Pomerans, John Shepley, & Krishna Winston. New York, NY: Pantheon Books.

Celenza, Andrea (2007). *Sexual Boundary Violations: Therapeutic, Supervisory, and Academic Contexts.* New York, NY: Aronson.

Cesio, Fidias (1993). "The Oedipal Tragedy in the Psychoanalytic Process: Transference Love." In *On Freud's "Observations on Transference-Love."* Ed. Ethel Spector Person, Aiban Hagelin, & Peter Fonagy. New Haven, CT: Yale University Press, 130–145.

Chetrit-Vatine, Viviane (2014). *The Ethical Seduction of the Psychoanalytic Situation: The Feminine-Maternal Origins of Responsibility for the Other.* Trans. Andrew Weller. London: Karnac.

Chiasson, Dan (2008, April 7). "Fast Company: The World of Frank O'Hara." *The New Yorker*, 85(8): 82–84.

Chodorow, Nancy (2010). "Beyond the Dyad: Individual Psychology, Social World." *Journal of the American Psychoanalytic Association*, 58: 207–230.

Davies, Jody Messler (1994). "Love in the Afternoon: A Relational Reconsideration of Desire and Dread in the Countertransference." *Psychoanalytic Dialogues*, 4: 153–170.

Dimen, Muriel (2011). "*Lapsus Linguae*, or a Slip of the Tongue? A Sexual Violation in an Analytic Treatment and its Personal and Theoretical Aftermath." *Contemporary Psychoanalysis*, 47: 35–79.

Ehrenberg, Darlene (1992). *The Intimate Edge.* New York, NY: W. W. Norton & Co.

Feinsilver, David (1998). "The Therapist as a Person Facing Death: The Hardest of External Realities and Therapeutic Action." *International Journal of Psychoanalysis*, 79: 1131–1150.

Fergusson, Francis (1949). *The Idea of a Theater.* Princeton, NJ: Princeton University Press.

Fliess, Robert (1942). "The Metapsychology of the Analyst." *Psychoanalysis Quarterly*, 11: 211–227.

Forrester, John (1990). *The Seductions of Psychoanalysis: Freud, Lacan and Derrida.* Cambridge: Cambridge University Press.

Frank, Jerome D. & Frank, Julia B. (1961). *Persuasion and Healing: A Comparative Study of Psychotherapy.* Baltimore: Johns Hopkins University Press.

Freedman, Abraham (1990). "Death of the Psychoanalyst as a Form of Termination of Psychoanalysis." In *Illness in the Analyst: Implications for the Treatment Relationship.* Ed. Harvey J. Schwartz & Ann-Louise Silver. Madison, CT: International Universities Press, 299–331.

Freud, Anna (1966 [1936]). *The Ego and the Mechanisms of Defense.* Rev. ed. New York, NY: International Universities Press.

Freud, Anna & Burlingham, Dorothy (1943). *War and Children.* New York, NY: Medical War Books.

Freud, Sigmund (1893). Charcot. *S. E. 3:9–23.* London: Hogarth Press.

— (1905). Psychical (or Mental) Treatment. *S. E., 7:283–302.* London: Hogarth Press.

— (1907). Delusions and Dreams in Jensen's *Gradiva. S. E., 9:7–96.* London: Hogarth Press.

— (1908). Creative Writers and Day-Dreaming. *S. E., 9:141–154.* London: Hogarth Press.

— (1910). Five Lectures on Psycho-Analysis. *S. E., 11:9–55.* London: Hogarth Press.

— (1912a). The Dynamics of Transference. *S. E., 12:97–108.* London: Hogarth Press.

— (1912b). On the Universal Tendency to Debasement in the Sphere of Love. *S. E., 11:179–190.* London: Hogarth Press.

— (1912c). Recommendations to Physicians Practising Psycho-Analysis. *S. E., 12:109–120.* London: Hogarth Press.

— (1914a). On Narcissism: An Introduction. *S. E., 12:67–102.* London: Hogarth Press.

— (1914b). Remembering, Repeating and Working-Through. *S. E., 12:145–156.* London: Hogarth Press.

— (1915a). Observations on Transference-Love. *S. E., 12:159–171.* London: Hogarth Press.

— (1915b). Thoughts for the Times on War and Death. *S. E.,* 14:273–300. London: Hogarth Press.

— (1916a). On Transience. *S. E., 14:303–307.* London: Hogarth Press.

— (1916b). Some Character-Types Met with in Psycho-Analytic Work: I. The "Exceptions." *S. E., 14:311–316.* London: Hogarth Press.

— (1916–1917). Introductory Lectures on Psycho-Analysis. *S. E., 15–16:3–496.* London: Hogarth Press.

— (1917 [1915]). Mourning and Melancholia. *S. E., 14:239–258.* London: Hogarth Press.

— (1920). Beyond the Pleasure Principle. *S. E., 18:1–64.* London: Hogarth Press.

— (1926). The Question of Lay-Analysis: Conversations with an Impartial Person. *S. E., 20:183–250.* London: Hogarth Press.

— (1930). Civilization and Its Discontents. *S. E., 21:64–145.* London: Hogarth Press.

— (1937). Analysis Terminable and Interminable. *S. E., 23:216–253.* London: Hogarth Press.

— (1940). An Outline of Psycho-Analysis. *S. E., 23:141–207.* London: Hogarth Press.

Friedman, Lawrence (1988). *The Anatomy of Psychotherapy.* Hillsdale, NJ: The Analytic Press.

— (1991). "On the Therapeutic Action of Loewald's Theory." In *The Work of Hans Loewald: An Introduction and Commentary*. Ed. Gerald I. Fogel. Northvale, NJ: Aronson, 91–104.

— (1997). "Ferrum, Ignis, and Medicina: Return to the Crucible." *Journal of the American Psychoanalytic Association*, 45: 20–36.

— (2005). "Psychoanalytic Treatment: Thick Soup or Thin Gruel?" *Psychoanalytic Inquiry*, 25: 418–439.

— (2006). "What Is Psychoanalysis?" *Psychoanalytic Quarterly*, 75: 689–713.

— (2008a). "A Renaissance for Freud's *Papers on Technique.*" *Psychoanalytic Quarterly*, 77: 1031–1044.

— (2008b). "Loewald." *Journal of the American Psychoanalytic Association*, 56: 1105–1115.

Gabbard, Glen (1997). "Discussion." *Psychoanalytic Inquiry*, 17: 371–386.

— (2009). "What Is a 'Good Enough' Termination?" *Journal of the American Psychoanalytic Association*, 57: 575–594.

Gabbard, Glen & Lester, Eva (1995). *Boundaries and Boundary Violations in Psychoanalysis*. New York, NY: Basic Books.

Gardner, M. Robert (1983). *Self Inquiry*. Boston, MA: Little, Brown.

Green, André (1972). *On Private Madness*. Madison, CT: International Universities Press.

Green, André (2005). *Key Ideas for Contemporary Psychoanalysis: Misrecognition and Recognition of the Unconscious*. Trans. Andrew Weller. General Ed. Dana Birksted-Breen. London: Routledge.

Greenberg, Jay (1995). "Psychoanalytic Technique and the Interactive Matrix." *Psychoanalytic Quarterly*, 64: 1–22.

Greenblatt, Stephen (1997). "Commentary on *A Midsummer Night's Dream.*" In *The Norton Shakespeare*. Ed. Stephen Greenblatt. New York, NY: Norton, 805–814.

Greenson, Ralph & Wexler, Milton (1969). "The Non-Transference Relationship in the Psychoanalytic Situation." *International Journal of Psychoanalysis*, 50: 27–40.

Grossman, William (1992). "Comments on the Concept of the 'Analyzing Instrument.'" *Journal of Clinical Psychoanalysis*, 1: 261–271.

Heaney, Seamus (1990). Sonnet V, from "Clearances." In *Opened Ground: Selected Poems 1966–1996*. New York, NY: Farrar, Straus and Giroux.

Heimann, Paula (1950). "On Counter-Transference." *International Journal of Psychoanalysis*, 31: 81–84.

— (1956). "Dynamics of Transference Interpretations." *International Journal of Psychoanalysis*, 37: 303–310.

Hernandez, Max (1993). "Footnote to a Footnote to 'Observations on Transference-Love.'" In *On Freud's "Observations on Transference-Love."*

Ed. Ethel Spector Person, Aiban Hagelin, & Peter Fonagy. New Haven, CT: Yale University Press, 96–101.

Hoffer, Axel (1993). "Is Love in the Analytic Relationship 'Real'?" *Psychoanalytical Inquiry*, 13: 343–356.

Hoffman, Irwin (1983). "The Patient as Interpreter of the Analyst's Experience." *Contemporary Psychoanalysis* 19: 389–422.

Homer (1965). *The Odyssey*. Trans. Emile Victor Rieu. Harmondsworth, England: Penguin Classics.

Hughes, Judith (2004). *From Obstacle to Ally: The Evolution of Psychoanalytic Practice*. New York, NY: Brunner Routledge.

Isakower, Otto (1963). New York Psychoanalytic Institute. *Minutes of the Faculty Meeting* October 14–November 20. Unpublished.

Jones, Alice (2013). "'Now We're out of Time': Thoughts on Endings in Poetry and Psychoanalysis." *American Imago*, 70(4): 606–632.

Kantrowitz, Judy (2015). *Myths of Termination: What Patients Can Teach Psychoanalysts about Endings*. London: Routledge.

Kahr, Brett (2015). "Winnicott's *Anni Horribiles*: The Biographical Roots of 'Hate in the Counter-Transference.'" In *The Winnicott Tradition: Lines of Development—Evolution of Theory and Practice over the Decades*. Ed. Margaret Boyle Spelman and Frances Thomson-Salo. London: Karnac, 69–84.

Kerr, John (1993). *A Most Dangerous Method*. New York, NY: Knopf.

Khan, Masud (1973). "The Role of Illusion in the Analytic Space and Process." *Annual of Psychoanalysis*, 1: 231–246.

Klauber, John (1981). "The Identity of the Psychoanalyst." In *Difficulties in the Analytic Encounter*. New York, NY: Jason Aronson, 161–180.

Kohon, Gregorio (1984). "Reflections on Dora: The Case of Hysteria." *International Journal of Psychoanalysis*, 65: 73–84.

Kubie, Lawrence (1968). "Unsolved Problems in the Resolution of the Transference." *Psychoanalytic Quarterly*, 37: 331–352.

Landor, Walter (1936). *The Complete Works of Walter Savage Landor*, *Vol. 16*. Ed. Stephen Wheeler. London: Chapman and Hall.

Levine, Frederic (2003). "The Forbidden Quest and the Slippery Slope: Roots of Authoritarianism in Psychoanalysis." *Journal of the American Psychoanalytic Association*, 51 (Suppl.): 203–245.

Levine, Howard (1997a). "Prologue." *Psychoanalytic Inquiry*, 17: 237–241.

— (1997b). "Epilogue: Sexual Trauma: Where Do We Stand?" *Psychoanalytic Inquiry*, 17: 387–391.

— (2010). "Sexual Boundary Violations: A Psychoanalytic Perspective." *British Journal of Psychotherapy*, 26: 50–63.

Loewald, Hans W. (1971). "The Transference Neurosis: Comments on the Concept and the Phenomenon." In *Papers on Psychoanalysis*. New Haven, CT: Yale University Press, 302–314.

— (1975). "Psychoanalysis as an Art and the Fantasy Character of the Psychoanalytic Situation." *Journal of the American Psychoanalytic Association*, 23: 277–299.

— (1978). "Primary Process, Secondary Process, and Language." In *Papers on Psychoanalysis*. New Haven, CT: Yale University Press, 1980, 178–206.

— (1980 [1960]). "On the Therapeutic Action of Psychoanalysis." In *Papers on Psychoanalysis*. New Haven, CT: Yale University Press, 221–256.

— (1980 [1970]). "Psychoanalytic Theory and the Psychoanalytic Process." In *Papers on Psychoanalysis*. New Haven, CT: Yale University Press, 277–299.

— (1986). "Transference-Countertransference." *Journal of the American Psychoanalytic Association*, 34: 275–287.

— (2000 [1988]). "Sublimation: Inquiries into Theoretical Psychoanalysis." In *The Essential Loewald: Collected Papers and Monographs*. Hagerstown, MD: University Publishing, 439–527.

Lord, Ruth, Ritvo, Samuel, & Solnit, Albert (1978). "Patients' Reactions to the Death of the Psychoanalyst." *International Journal of Psychoanalysis*, 59: 189–197.

Macalpine, Ida (1950). "The Development of Transference." *Psychoanalytic Quarterly*, 19: 501–539.

Margolis, Marvin (1997). "Analyst-Patient Sexual Involvement." *Psychoanalytic Inquiry*, 17: 349–370.

McGuire, William (Ed.) (1974). *The Freud/Jung Letters: The Correspondence between Sigmund Freud and C. G. Jung*. Trans. Ralph Mannheim & R. C. F. Hull. Cambridge, MA: Harvard University Press, 1988.

McLaughlin, James (1981). "Transference, Psychic Reality, and Countertransference." *Psychoanalytic Quarterly*, 50: 639–664.

Meisel, Perry & Kendrick, Walter (Eds.) (1985). *Bloomsbury/Freud: The Letters of James and Alix Strachey, 1924–1925*. New York, NY: Basic Books.

Modell, Arnold (1991). "The Therapeutic Relationship as a Paradoxical Experience." *Psychoanalytic Dialogues*, 1: 13–28.

Morrison, Amy (1990). "Ten Years of Doing Psychotherapy with a Life-Threatening Illness." In *Illness in the Analyst: Implications for the Treatment Relationship*. Ed. Harvey J. Schwartz & Ann-Louise Silver. Madison, CT: International Universities Press, 227–250.

Neruda, Pablo (1993). "Childhood and Poetry." In *Neruda and Vallejo: Selected Poems*. Trans. Robert Bly. Boston, MA: Beacon Press.

Nestrick, William (1975). "George Herbert—the Giver and the Gift." *Ploughshares*, 2: 187–205.

Ogden, Thomas (1994). *Subjects of Analysis*. Northvale, NJ: Jason Aronson.

— (1997). *Reverie and Interpretation*. Northvale, NJ: Jason Aronson.

Orgel, Shelly (1997). "Commentary on Friedman." *Journal of the American Psychoanalytic Association*, 45:57–61.

Pick, Irma Brenman (1985). "Working through in the Countertransference." *International Journal of Psychoanalysis*, 66: 157–166.

Pinsky, Ellen (2002). "Mortal Gifts: A Two-Part Essay on the Therapist's Mortality." *Journal of the American Academy of Psychoanalysis & Dynamic Psychiatry*, 30: 173–204.

— (2008). "Loewald Panel: Discussion." *Journal of the American Psychoanalytic Association*, 56: 1129–1137.

— (2011). "The Olympian Delusion." *Journal of the American Psychoanalytic Association*, 59: 351–375.

— (2012). "Physic Himself Must Fade: A View of the Therapeutic Offering through the Lens of Mortality." *American Imago*, 69: 29–56.

— (2014a). "Mortality, Integrity, and Psychoanalysis (Who are you to me? Who am I to you?)." *Psychoanalytic Quarterly*, 83: 1–22.

— (2014b) "The Potion: Reflections on Freud's 'Observations on Transference-Love.'" *Journal of the American Psychoanalytic Association*, 62: 455–474.

Poland, Warren (1996 [1984]). "The Analyst's Neutrality." In *Melting the Darkness*. Northvale, NJ: Jason Aronson, 85–100.

— (1996 [1988]). "Insight and the Analytic Dyad." In *Melting the Darkness*. Northvale, NJ: Jason Aronson, 55–81.

— (2000). "The Analyst's Witnessing and Otherness." *Journal of the American Psychoanalytic Association*, 48: 17–34.

Rangell, Leo (1996). "The 'Analytic' in Psychoanalytic Treatment: How Analysis Works." *Psychoanalytic Inquiry*, 16: 140–166.

Renik, Owen (1993a). "Analytic Interaction: Conceptualizing Technique in Light of the Analyst's Irreducible Subjectivity." *Psychoanalytic Quarterly*, 62: 553–571.

— (1993b). "Countertransference Enactment and the Psychoanalytic Process." In *Psychic Structure and Psychic Change: Essays in Honor of Robert S. Wallerstein, M. D.* Ed. Mardi Horowitz, Otto Kernberg, & Edward Weinshel. Madison, CT: International Universities Press, 137–160.

Rizzuto, Ana-Maria (1995). "Sound and Sense: Words in Psychoanalysis and the Paradox of the Suffering Person." *Canadian Journal of Psychoanalysis*, 3: 1–15.

Roud, Richard (1980). "Jean Renoir to 1939." In *Cinema: A Critical Dictionary, Volume Two*. Ed. Richard Roud. New York, NY: Viking, 835–845.

Samuels, Laurel (1992). "When the Analyst Cannot Continue." *The San Francisco Jung Institute Library Journal*, 10: 27–38.

Schwartz, Harvey & Silver, Ann-Louise (Eds.) (1990). *Illness in the Analyst: Implications for the Treatment Relationship.* Madison, CT: International Universities Press.

Shengold, Leonard (1991). *"Father, Don't You See I'm Burning?": Reflections on Sex, Narcissism, Symbolism, and Murder: From Everything to Nothing.* New Haven, CT: Yale University Press.

Simon, Bennett (1992). "'Incest—See Under Oedipus Complex': The History of an Error in Psychoanalysis." *Journal of the American Psychoanalytic Association*, 40: 955–988.

Smee, Sebastian (2015). "A Colorful View of a Lost Empire." *The Boston Globe*, November 30, 2015, G3.

Smith, Henry (2006). "Love and Other Monsters: An Introduction." *Psychoanalytic Quarterly*, 75: 685–688.

Spillius, Elizabeth Bott (2001). "Freud and Klein on the Concept of Phantasy." *International Journal of Psychoanalysis*, 82: 361–373.

Stoller, Robert J. (1975). *Perversion: The Erotic Form of Hatred.* New York, NY: Pantheon Books.

Stone, Leo (1961). *The Psychoanalytic Situation.* New York, NY: International Universities Press.

Strachey, James (1934). "The Nature of the Therapeutic Action of Psychoanalysis." *International Journal of Psychoanalysis*, 15: 127–159.

Szasz, Thomas (1963). "The Concept of Transference." *International Journal of Psychoanalysis*, 44: 432–443.

Tarachow, Sidney (1962). "Interpretation and Reality in Psychotherapy." *International Journal of Psychoanalysis*, 43: 377–387.

— (1963). *An Introduction to Psychotherapy.* New York, NY: International Universities Press.

Thompson, Michael Guy (2004). *The Ethic of Honesty: The Fundamental Rule of Psychoanalysis.* Contemporary Psychoanalytic Studies 2. Amsterdam: Rodopi.

Traesdal, Tove (2005). "When the Analyst Dies: Dealing with the Aftermath." *Journal of the American Psychoanalytic Association*, 53: 1235–1255.

Von Unwerth, Matthew (2005). *Freud's Requiem: Mourning, Memory, and the Invisible History of a Summer Walk.* New York, NY: Riverhead Books.

Weil, Simone (1963). *Gravity and Grace.* London: Routledge.

Winnicott, Donald Woods (1941). "The Observation of Infants in a Set Situation." *International Journal of Psychoanalysis*, 22: 229–249.

— (1949). "Hate in the Counter-Transference." *International Journal of Psychoanalysis*, 30: 69–74.

— (1960). "Counter-Transference." In *The Maturational Processes and the Facilitating Environment: Studies in the Theory of Emotional Development* (1965 ed.). New York, NY: International Universities Press, 158–165.

— (1962). "The Aims of Psycho-Analytic Treatment." In *The Maturational Processes and the Facilitating Environment: Studies in the Theory of Emotional Development* (1965 ed.). New York: International Universities Press, 166–170.

— (1963). "Communicating and Not Communicating Leading to a Study of Certain Opposites." In *The Maturational Processes and the Facilitating Environment*. Madison, CT: International Universities Press, 179–192.

— (1969). "The Use of an Object." *International Journal of Psychoanalysis*, 50: 711–716.

— (1971). *Playing and Reality*. London: Tavistock.

Wohlberg, Janet (1997). "Sexual Abuse in the Therapeutic Setting: What Do Victims Really Want?" *Psychoanalytic Inquiry*, 17: 329–348.

Young-Bruehl, Elisabeth (1988). *Anna Freud: A Biography*. New Haven, CT: Yale University Press.

— (2009). "Psychobiography and Character Study: A Reflection." Paper presented to the Psychoanalytic Institute and Society of New England, East, February 21.

Index

Abraham, Karl 20
abstinence, 47; as alluring 34, 56;
  magnetic 49; promise of 49
affect, analyst's management of 60
Almond, Richard 11, 18–19
Anna Freud: A Biography 45
Aurelius, Marcus 69

Bergmann, Martin 44
Beyond the Pleasure Principle 74–5
Boccaccio 110
*Boundaries and Boundary Violations
  in Psychoanalysis* 54–5
boundary violation 42
Breuer, Josef 35
Bulfinch, Thomas 43
Burlingham, Dorothy 45, 48, 69

Calef, Victor 57
"catalytic ferment" 8, 17
Cesio, Fidias 33, 51, 56
Charcot 20
charismatic style, rejection of 121
Chetrit-Vatine, Viviane 34
Chiasson, Dan 90
Chodorow, Nancy 11
classical position 105
countertransference 66, 93, 96,
  101, 112

da Vinci, Leonardo 107
death and fallibility in the
  psychoanalytic encounter,
  introduction to 1–5; analyst's
  mortal imperfection 3; forgetting
  3; mortality 2, 5; talking cure
  1–2
death of therapist 16, 114, 119
dreaming 37

enchanted glass 25, 93
ending of therapeutic relationship
  6–25; abstinence, fundamental
  paradox of 10; "affect-filled
  silence" 16; analyst retaliation
  16; audacious endeavor 12;
  built-in loss 21; "catalytic
  ferment" 8, 17; chemistry analogy
  8; countertransference 19;
  "enchanted glass" 25; grandiosity
  23; "highly explosive forces"
  9; humanness 7; "keeper of the
  analytic process" 21; metaphor 23;
  patient's mourning 22; presence,
  forms of 19; "specialness" 19;
  "technical device" 11; transference
  7, 9
erotic feelings 31
evocative language 116

Ferenczi, Sandor 51
Fergusson, Francis 80
Fliess, Robert 62
Forrester, John 35
Frank, Jerome 18
free associations 103
Freud, Anna 42, 45–6, 49, 69, 99
Freud, Sigmund 1, 4, 20, 23, 26–7,
    29–31, 33, 35–6, 40, 44, 46, 59,
    61, 63, 69, 72, 80–1, 83, 92, 94,
    97, 102–3, 107, 109, 116
Friedman, Lawrence 3, 33, 35, 44,
    92–3
Friedman, Manna 67

Gabbard, Glen 40, 52
Gardner, Robert 15, 24
Goethe 69, 86
Green, André 14, 27, 47, 71, 73, 85
Greenberg, Jay 98
Greenblatt, Stephen 31

Harbach, Otto 36
Heaney, Seamus 90–1, 92
Heimann, Paula 26–7, 32
Hernandez, Max 29, 39
Hoffman, Irwin 96

The Idea of a Theater 80
Illness in the Analyst 20
infant: aggression 84; observation
    of 78
instrument 69–91; adult version
    of play 80; "art as reparation"
    79; asymmetrical situation 70;
    "benevolent neutrality" 73;
    ceremony 80; clinical instrument
    83; clinical situation 69, 72;
    dangers of the psychoanalytic
    situation 87; form 71, 88; hazard
    86; incivility, form of 84; infant

aggression 84; infants, observation
    of 78; "instrument of research"
    76; limits imposed by form 84;
    looming destruction 89; loss 75,
    83; mourning 70, 89; nursery scene
    75; phantasies 81; rationalistic
    extreme 90; realm of fiction 72;
    scarcity 83, 88; transference
    paradox 88; trust 82; value 83, 85;
    working-through 70, 73
Isakower, Otto 103

Jones, Alice 90
Jonson, Ben 70, 82, 92
Jung, Carl 51, 64, 67

Kantrowitz, Judy 62
Kern, Jerome 36
Kernberg, Otto 59
Khan, Masud 30
Kierkegaard 46
Klauber, John 27, 89
Klein, Melanie 27
Kubie, Lawrence 87

Landor, Walter Savage 6
language, "magical-evocative"
    function of 115
Levine, Howard 52, 100
Loewald, Hans W. 16, 26, 32, 41,
    73, 79, 87, 98, 105–6
Lord, Ruth 95

Macalpine, Ida 10, 27, 34, 55
Margolis, Marvin 52
McGuire, William 66
McLaughlin, James 104
A Midsummer Night's Dream 31, 39
mirrors and monsters 92–116;
    analyst as creature of shifting
    shape 99; analytic instrument

104; analytic terms, purpose of
93; classical position 105; closed
system 105; countertransference
93, 96, 101, 112; death of therapist
114; differentiation of positions
98; doctor's "coming to grief"
112; emotional involvement
of analyst 96; enchanted glass
93; enterprise 92; essential
vocabulary of now-endangered
creatures 94; examples 103; free
associations 103; "good sex,"
disclaimer regarding 102; heroic
role for the analyst 94; historical
progression 103; imperfection
and mortality 115; language,
"magical-evocative" function
of 115; line between acceptable
and exploitative 109; metaphors
and similes 94; "more" 106;
"no model" 92; opposites 102;
patient's grief 112; plunging-along
analyst 108; redemption 115;
safe-keeping 107, 116; self-aware
human presence 98; therapeutic
relationship, what is unique to
95; tightrope image 97, 100;
transference 93, 115; treatment
artifice 108
Modell, Arnold 62
mortal gift, therapeutic offering as
5, 40
mourning 70, 89

Nashe, Thomas 6
Nemetz, Joseph 119
Neruda, Pablo 114, 119
Nestrick, William 4

Ogden, Thomas 71
old terms 94

Olympian delusion 44, 59, 113
Orgel, Shelly 42

Palos, Elma 51
Papers on Technique 3, 13, 44, 55,
60, 64, 96, 109
phantasies 81
Pick, Irma Brenman 96–8
Pinsky, Ellen 58
play, adult version of 80
pleased assumption 120
plunging-along analyst 108
Poland, Warren 73, 107–8
potion 26–43; abstinence, allure
of 34; boundary violation 42;
conflagration 26; dreaming
37; erotic feelings 31; "highly
explosive forces" 33; idealized
image of a mirror 26; "irruption
of reality" 29; "moment of
forgetfulness" 43; "potion-
diluter" 42; profound paradox
34; seduction 38; transference,
temptations embedded in power of
39; transformed vision 36

Rangell, Leo 104–5
Renik, Owen 101
Renoir, Jean 26
Richard III 48
Ritvo, Samuel 95
Rizzuto, Ana Maria 15, 94
Roud, Richard 26
The Rules of the Game 26

safe-keeping 107, 116
Samuels, Laurel 20
"saz" style 93
Schwartz, Harvey 20
self-aware human presence 98
sexual exploitation of patients

44–67; abstinence, promise of
49; abstinence as alluring 56;
affect, analyst's management
of 60; analyst's silence 57;
countertransference 66; latent
truths 46; metaphor 46; mixed
metaphors 60; myths 63;
"occupational hazard" for the
therapist 56; Olympian delusion
59; pedagogical bond 61; pledge
of candor 47, 49; "psychical
(mental) treatment" 47; "rare
and exalted perfection" 62; risks
inherent to the psychoanalytic
exchange 64; self-effacement 63;
self-help group for women 53;
superhuman, therapist elevated
to 62; touch 45; "virtuoso
sublimator" 50; "working
through" 59
Shakespeare, William 2, 6, 7, 90
Shengold, Leonard 63
Silver, Ann-Louise 20
Simmel, George 11
Simon, Bennett 50
Smee, Sebastian 93
Solnit, Albert 95
Spielrein, Sabina 64, 111
Stoller, Robert J. 42

Stone, Leo 47, 73, 78, 87, 95
Strachey, Alix 20
Strachey, James 96
superhuman, therapist elevated
to 62
Swift, Jonathan 72
Szasz, Thomas 57, 86–7

talking cure 1–2
Tarachow, Sidney 32, 97
Thompson, Guy 58, 60
tightrope image 97, 100
transference: definition of 93;
development of 7; love 18;
mirror and shield provided by
24; "neurosis" 115; paradox 88;
power of, temptations embedded
in 39; range of feelings
experienced in 18; as universal
phenomenon 9; see also potion

Weil, Simone 74
Weinshel, Edward 57
Winnicott, Donald Woods 7, 12–13,
17, 27, 57, 71, 76–9, 84, 87
Wohlberg, Janet 53
working-through 59, 70, 73

Young-Bruehl, Elisabeth 45–6, 48